AIR WAR IN VIETNAM

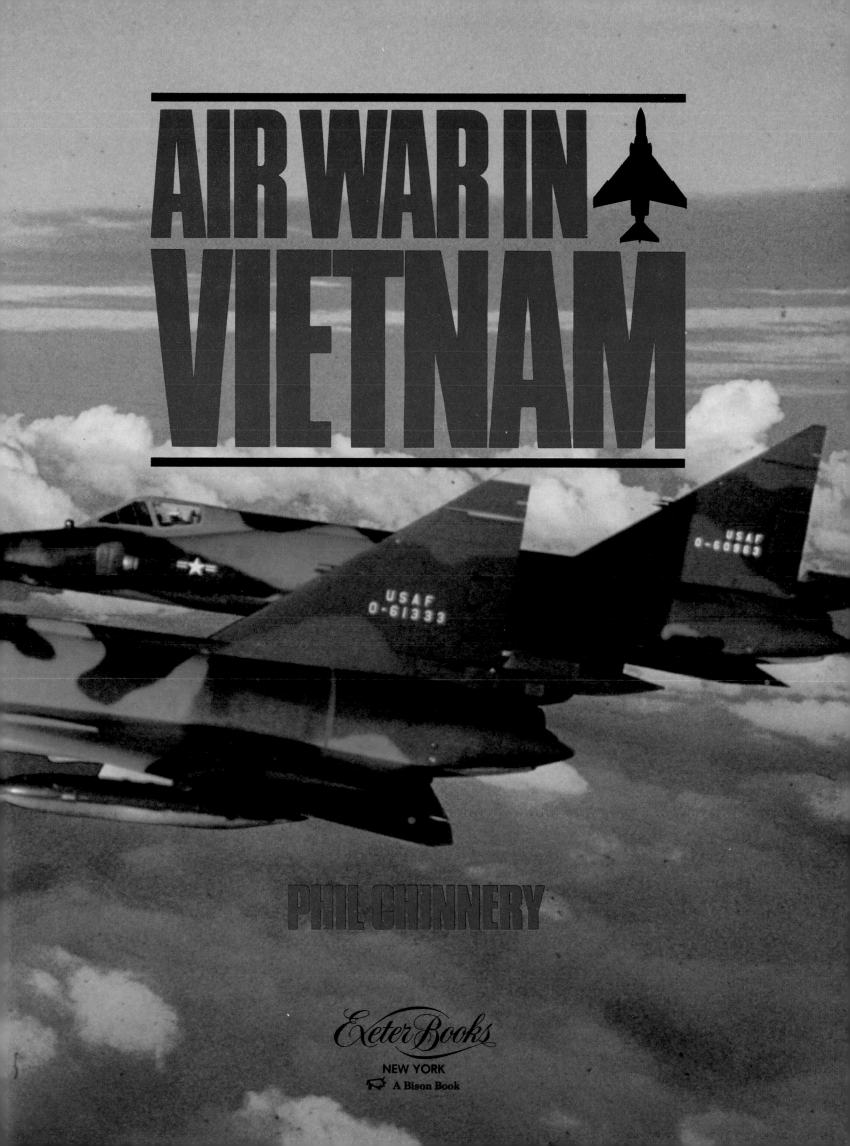

AIR WAR IN VIETNAM

PHIL CHINNERY

Exeter Books

NEW YORK
A Bison Book

First published in USA 1987
by Exeter Books
Distributed by Bookthrift
Exeter is a trademark of
Bookthrift Marketing, Inc.
Bookthrift is a registered trademark of
Bookthrift Marketing
New York, New York

ISBN 0-671-08927-7

Printed in Hong Kong

PAGE 1: F-4C Phantoms on their way to bomb targets in the North in 1965.
PAGES 2-3: F-102A Delta Dagger interceptors were based in South Vietnam from 1962-69.
THIS PAGE: An A-1E Skyraider ready for launch from the *Intrepid* in the Gulf of Tonkin in 1967.

The author would like to thank the following for their assistance in the preparation of this book: Robert F Dorr, Lou Drendel, Mike J Kasiuba, Bob Livingstone, Col Bruce Martin (USMC (Ret), Peter Mersky, John B Morgan III, Dr John Pote, Nick Williams, Jim Wood, Randy Zahn, Embassy of the Socialist Republic of Vietnam, 1st Lt June Green and Lt Col Joseph Wagovich of the USAF Magazines and Books Division.
Acknowledgments for individual photographs are listed on page 192.

CONTENTS

1. The Early Years

From 1965 onwards, television news programs often showed captured American pilots being paraded through the streets of Hanoi en route to the infamous Hoa Lo prison. Had those same pilots been downed over North Vietnam two decades earlier they would have received an entirely different reception. United States involvement in Vietnam originally began as long ago as 1945. American pilots were flying combat missions against the Japanese who had occupied French Indochina during World War II and their B-24 Liberator bombers were being shot down over the same terrain that F-105 Thunderchiefs would be, 20 years later.

In an attempt to recover downed US aircrews, agents of the Office of Strategic Services (OSS) were parachuted into the hills of Annam toward the end of the war, to train and arm local guerrilla bands. These guerrillas would help search for American pilots and attempt to cut rail lines used by the Japanese. They were led by a man known as Ho Chi Minh.

Ho was a Marxist-Leninist who had formed the Indochinese Communist Party in 1930, but to the Vietnamese nationalist groups who were fighting to rid their country not only of the Japanese, but the French as well, Ho appeared to have American backing and they turned to him as their leader. As the war came to an end the Japanese were disarmed and with the French colonial overseers weak and disorganized, a vacuum existed which Ho Chi Minh was quick to fill. Ho's American-trained guerrillas, known as the Viet Minh, marched into Hanoi and with a groundswell of popular support formed a Provisional Government. The Emperor Bao Dai abdicated on 30 August 1945 and two days later Ho Chi Minh's Nationalist forces issued a declaration of independence establishing the Democratic Republic of Vietnam.

In October the OSS teams were withdrawn following the death of an OSS officer who was shot at a Viet Minh roadblock. The officer, Major Peter Dewey, was the first American to die in the Vietnam war. Within months a well-armed French expeditionary corps of three full divisions had begun to arrive and the Viet Minh once again prepared for war.

The French were determined to regain control of their former colony, but Ho Chi Minh was a worthy adversary. When the negotiations broke down in Paris in October 1946 he ordered his 60,000 troops into the countryside to prepare for a protracted guerrilla war.

Fighting broke out between the Viet Minh and French troops in December 1946 and continued until June 1949 when the situation was at a stalemate, despite the presence of over 150,000 French troops. At this time China fell to Mao's communist troops and the Viet Minh found themselves with an ally on their northern border who was willing to train them and supply large quantities of arms and ammunition.

In Europe, where most of the Eastern European countries had fallen under Soviet control, America had begun to assist France to return to her pre-war status in Western Europe. This support was also extended to French policy in Indochina where France proposed to give only limited autonomy to Vietnam, Laos and Cambodia.

As the guerrilla war gathered momentum France had to commit ever increasing military resources to Indochina. On 16 February 1950 France formally requested American military and economic assistance to help to defeat the Viet Minh. The Truman administration concluded that 'the threat of Communist aggression in Indochina is only one phase of anticipated Communist plans to seize all of Southeast Asia' and in May material as

PAGES 6-7: Vietnamese Air Force C-47s being loaded with supplies at Saigon.
BELOW: General Vo Nguyen Giap (left), commander of the Viet Minh and the legendary Ho Chi Minh stand together in 1945.

8

well as financial assistance was approved by President Truman.

In the summer of 1950 the United States established a Military Assistance Advisory Group (MAAG) in Saigon and military advisers began to arrive to assist the French wherever possible. Air Force advisers and engineers were used in particular to help maintain American-supplied aircraft, of which over 500 were eventually delivered. These included Douglas C-47 transport aircraft and Grumman F8F Bearcat fighters, the latter taken from United States Navy and Marine Air Reserve squadrons.

Toward the end of 1950 the now well-armed Viet Minh went on the offensive and French casualties began to increase. In December the US-supplied aircraft dropped napalm for the first

RIGHT: General Navarre inspects French and Vietnamese troops at Dien Bien Phu.
BELOW: Viet Minh guerrillas at Dien Bien Phu rejoice on the wreck of a French C-47.

time on Viet Minh troops operating near Tien Yen. A terrifying, if spectacular weapon, napalm explodes on impact and sends a wall of flame across the ground, incinerating everything in its path.

In 1951 the French decided to create a Vietnamese national army including a small air-component known as the Air Department of the Joint General Staff. A flight training center was established at the coastal air base of Nha Trang to teach Vietnamese personnel to fly and to train the necessary ground staff to support the new air unit. By the end of the year the 1st Air Observation Squadron (AOS) had been formed, flying the Morane Saulnier MS.500 Criquet, the French-built derivative of the Fieseler Storch. The Criquet was the standard equipment for most of the French Air Force observation squadrons in Indochina and soon the 1st AOS began operating with French units against the Viet Minh in southern Vietnam. The French Air Force made little effort to develop a self-sufficient Vietnamese air unit and used the Vietnamese only as replacements within their own squadrons.

Following the formation of a second observation squadron at Hue in 1952, flying the Criquet, a number of light transport aircraft were supplied, including Beechcraft C-45's and Republic Seabee amphibians. These aircraft were used to equip the 1st Liaison Squadron, based at Saigon's municipal airport, Tan Son Nhut. This unit was used to shuttle personnel and supplies along the coast between Hue and Saigon.

The Vietnamese government then requested additional aircraft to equip a combat unit, but the best that the French could offer was the relatively docile, twin engined light transport aircraft, the Dassault MD-315 Flamant, fitted with bomb racks.

The increase in aircraft and manpower began to tax the training facility at Nha Trang, so prospective bomber and transport pilots were sent overseas for training, which began with two months schooling in light aircraft in France. This was followed by a year in Morocco learning to fly the North American T-6, and then back to France for four more months training in the Flamant. By the spring of 1954 the first squadron of 16 Flamant bombers was operational and flying missions along-

side French Air Force Douglas B-26 Invaders and F8F Bearcats.

While the fledgling Vietnamese Air Force (VNAF) was struggling to establish itself, the war was going badly for the French. By the summer of 1953 the Viet Minh had crossed the border into Laos and set up a revolutionary Pathet Lao government in the capital Luang Prabang. During their drive toward Laos the Viet Minh had overrun the French garrison and airfield at Dien Bien Phu in Northwestern Vietnam and it was here that the decisive battle of the first Vietnam war was to be fought.

General Henri Navarre, the French commander, decided to try to lure the Viet Minh to a set-piece battle where they could be annihilated by French airpower and massed artillery. In order to ensure that the elusive Viet Minh would attack, General Navarre planned to establish an impregnable fortress deep in enemy territory where it could threaten the Viet Minh lines of communication. Dien Bien Phu was chosen because of its location at the junction of

BELOW: Two unmarked Air America Caribou STOL transports unloading passengers and supplies at Sam Thong in Laos.

three main supply routes and its proximity to the border with Laos, ten miles away.

On 20 November 1953 Operation *Castor* began when 800 men of the French 1st Colonial Paratroop Battalion jumped out of 64 C-47 Skytrains over the village of Dien Bien Phu and landed among two companies of Viet Minh, which they then destroyed with the loss of 40 men. Soon 10,000 men were dug in around Dien Bien Phu, which lies in a valley about 180 miles from Hanoi, the nearest French air base.

Navarre's plan was basically sound, but it underestimated the ability of the Viet Minh to supply and reinforce its men around Dien Bien Phu, and it over-estimated the ability of the French Air Force to supply the base by air. General Giap, the Viet Minh commander, took up the challenge and encircled the base with 40,000 troops, outnumbering the reinforced 15,000 defenders by almost three to one. By the time the assault began the Viet Minh, using little more than sweat and muscle,

had dragged 200 artillery pieces into positions surrounding the base and within a few days the runway was cratered and unusable. French aircraft attempting to drop supplies to the shrinking garrison had to brave a murderous corridor of anti-aircraft fire and 48 aircraft were shot down during the 56 day assault.

Even at this early stage the American Central Intelligence Agency (CIA) was involved in activities in both North and South Vietnam. In an effort to assist the beleaguered French, their covert airline Civil Air Transport (CAT) was contracted to fly in supplies using twin-boom C-119 Flying Boxcar transports provided by the United States Air Force and flown by civilian crews. On one of the last supply-drops a C-119 being flown by two American pilots was hit by flak in the left wing and right boom and begun to lose altitude rapidly. Both pilots elected to stay with the plane as it lost height and eventually its left wing-tip dug into a hillside, the plane did a slow cartwheel and exploded in flame.

During the closing stages of the battle, American reconnaissance aircraft from an aircraft carrier task force in the South China Sea overflew the

area while American leaders discussed whether to intervene in the conflict. The commander of the US Far East Air Force Bomber Command flew over the battlefield in a B-17 and concluded that a B-29 bomber strike would be successful. Even the use of tactical nuclear weapons against the hills surrounding Dien Bien Phu was considered. Finally the President, no doubt influenced by the Korean war which had just ended, decided that the risks of intervention outweighed the potential gains. The French were on their own.

On 7 May 1954, having suffered over 7000 killed or wounded, the defenders of Dien Bien Phu surrendered to the Viet Minh whose own casualties were estimated at over 20,000 including 8000 killed. Eleven thousand French troops passed into captivity from which only half would return, due to lack of proper medical care, harsh conditions and inadequate food.

The defeat of the French army at Dien Bien Phu marked the beginning of the end of French influence in Indochina. The very next day at a previously scheduled international conference in Geneva, Switzerland, representatives of the major powers and of the Indo-

BELOW: Although the VNAF received their first Sikorsky H-34 helicopters in 1960, maintenance problems restricted their use.

chinese people met to discuss a cease fire agreement, which was subsequently approved on 20/21 July. The outcome of the agreement was that Vietnam would be divided along the 17th parallel into a communist North and a non-communist South; there would be a five mile demilitarized zone (DMZ) on either side of the border; French and Viet Minh forces would withdraw north and south of the DMZ and in two years elections would be held to decide the issue of reunification of the whole country.

The division of the country led to the establishment of two rival governments, in Hanoi in the North and Saigon in the South. Bao Dai had appointed Ngo Dinh Diem Premier in the South, in June 1954, and he set about creating separate armed forces, incorporating those that the French had formed in 1951. As a result the Vietnamese Air Force (VNAF) came into existence on 1 July 1955 as a separate entity, distinct from the Vietnamese

LEFT: An H-19 evacuates French wounded during the fighting at Dien Bien Phu.
BELOW: A Continental Air Services L382B Hercules unloading fuel and ammunition at the 1000 yard long TK-2 airfield in Laos.

General Staff, and with its own commander and staff.

At the time of its establishment the VNAF existed more in name than in reality. When Dien Bien Phu fell to the Viet Minh the VNAF consisted of only 58 aircraft and approximately 1345 personnel, concentrated at bases in Nha Trang, Da Nang, Bien Hoa and Tan Son Nhut. As they began to withdraw their forces the French replaced the VNAF Criquets with Cessna L-19 (later designated 0-1) Bird Dogs and the Flamants with Grumman Bearcats. The 25 Bearcats formed the 1st Fighter Squadron and were the first true combat aircraft that the VNAF had received. These were followed by 32 C-47 transports which were supplied under the Military Assistance Program (MAP) to equip the 1st Air Transport Group.

The United States decided to expand its influence in Indochina to try to contain the spread of communism and in February 1955 the Senate ratified the creation of the South East Asia Treaty Organisation (SEATO) whose eight members guaranteed the protection of

BELOW: A formation of Royal Thai Air Force Grumman F8F Bearcat fighters supplied from United States Navy stocks.

Laos, Cambodia and 'the free territory under the jurisdiction of the State of Vietnam.' In the same month, following a decision taken in October 1954, that the United States would provide aid directly to South Vietnam rather than through France, the 342 strong US Military Assistance Advisory Group (MAAG) began to assume responsibility for training the South Vietnamese Army.

In October 1955 President Diem set up an election within South Vietnam to decide whether the country should continue as a monarchy headed by Bao Dai, or as a Republic led by himself. The referendum was organized by Diem's brother Ngo Dinh Nhu and resulted in an unconvincing 99 percent vote in favor of the Republic.

The nationwide elections due to be held in July 1956 never took place. South Vietnam had not been a party to the French-Viet Minh agreement and argued that the northerners would not be able to vote freely under Ho Chi Minh's one-party rule and that the block vote of the North would overwhelm those cast in the South. The true reason for Diem's refusal may have been that although Ho was a communist, he was a legendary hero to the

Vietnamese people and would probably have won any nationwide election.

Ho Chi Minh had taken out insurance against the failure of the reunification elections to take place. During the ten months following the signing of the Geneva Agreement approximately 900,000 Vietnamese, mostly Catholics had resettled in the South, while 90,000 Viet Minh returned to the North. However, Ho had ordered 10,000 of his communist supporters to go to ground in South Vietnam and had buried arms to field 6000 guerrillas if the need arose.

The French continued to train the VNAF until May 1957 when American advisers took over. A basic flying school was set up at Nha Trang and Vietnamese cadets began receiving training on North American T-6 Texans, while others were sent to Clark Air Base in the Philippines or to the United States for more advanced training. More equipment began to arrive under MAP, including enough C-47s to form a second Transport Group and some replacement Bearcats. In March 1958 the first Sikorsky H-19 helicopters arrived and were formed into the 1st Helicopter Squadron. It was not long before the VNAF consisted of one fighter squadron (F8Fs), two transport

ABOVE: A C-47 of the Royal Lao Air Force at Saigon's Tan Son Nhut Air Base.
ABOVE LEFT: A C-47 of the 1st Transport Group ready for take off from Saigon.
BELOW LEFT: Royal Lao Air Force C-47s unload supplies in southern Laos.

squadrons (C-47s), two observation squadrons (L-19s) and one helicopter squadron (H-19s), with a number of T-6s and C-45s. Its primary mission was observation and transportation and as events were to prove, it was ill-equipped to deal with any threat posed by its communist neighbor in the North.

By the end of 1957 insurgent forces in the south, known by the derogatory name of Viet Cong (Vietnamese Communist) had begun to carry out terrorist acts against Diem's regime. One of their first targets was the US MAAG in Saigon which was bombed on 22 October 1957 injuring eight US servicemen. Individual acts of terrorism, such as kidnapping, bombing and murder, escalated and by the end of 1958 the Viet Cong had formed units of 50-200 men; had defeated a company of South Vietnamese regulars in an attack on a rubber plantation north of Saigon, and had attacked a government prison, releasing 50 suspected communists.

By May 1959 it had become obvious to the leaders in the North that their attempt to reunify the country through a nationwide election had failed and they announced that the country would be reunified by an armed struggle instead. Two months later a US Army major and master sergeant were killed during a Viet Cong attack on Bien Hoa Air Base and in September several Viet Cong companies ambushed a force of Army of the Republic of Vietnam (ARVN) troops on the marshy Plain of Reeds southwest of Saigon. According to the Viet Cong this incident marked the official start of the armed struggle.

The Viet Cong insurgency was becoming increasingly difficult for the South Vietnamese to contain. Supported by the North and aided by Diem's increasingly repressive rule, the strength of the Viet Cong grew and more American aid was requested. In October American officials asked for an increase in the strength of the MAAG from 342 men to 685, so as to provide more US Army Special Forces teams to train ARVN Rangers for border patrols. Despite communist protests to the International Control Commission (ICC) the request was approved and the additional Green Berets began to arrive.

Toward the end of 1959 a North Vietnamese Army (NVA) transportation group began work on the Ho Chi Minh Trail; an infiltration route from North Vietnam, through Laos and Cambodia, to the South. The trail became a series of tracks and roads running north to south along the Annamite mountains into Laos and fanning out into the jungles of South Vietnam. Soon the first of an initial 4500-man military cadre began to arrive in South Vietnam. They were mostly ethnic southerners who had received indoctrination and training in the north. These hard core Viet Cong were funneled into communist jungle base areas in Tay Ninh Province on the Cambodian border (later designated War Zone C by American officials); an area northwest of Saigon known as War Zone D and also into the dense U Minh forest area of the Ca Mau peninsula.

In the meantime the United States had not been idle. Major airfield construction efforts had commenced at Ubon, Udorn and Chiang Mai in

Thailand and new runways had been planned for the airfields at Vientiane and Tan Son Nhut.

By the summer of 1960 the VNAF was experiencing problems with its obsolete equipment. Its commander, Colonel Nguyen Xuan Vinh had been forced to ground all the Bearcats due to structural deficiencies. The United States responded by shipping the first of 25 former US Navy Douglas A-1 Skyraider aircraft to Vietnam in September to replace the F8Fs, and the first of 11 Sikorsky H-34 Choctaw helicopters arrived in December. Unfortunately spares and servicing problems kept many of the Skyraiders on the ground and similar problems were encountered by the H-34s which were supplied to improve ARVN mobility.

The Geneva Agreement of 1954 had conferred independence on the kingdoms of Cambodia and Laos as well as signalling the end of French rule in Vietnam. Throughout the following years, the Cambodian leader Prince Norodom Sihanouk walked a tightrope of neutrality and had to allow the communists to move supplies through his country, permit American bombing and ignore cross-border incursions from South Vietnam.

In Laos the situation was complicated to say the least. North Vietnam recognized the strategic importance of the country as a relatively safe infiltration route around the DMZ and into South Vietnam. After the Geneva Conference in 1954 around 7000 Viet Minh remained illegally in Laos and these formed the back-bone of the communist Pathet Lao guerrilla movement. By 1957 the Pathet Lao had won control over the mountain town of Tchepone from the weak Royal Lao Army. The town was the key crossroads of a trail network leading into South Vietnam's Central Highlands and the Mekong Delta, the 'rice bowl' of Vietnam.

America was forbidden by the Geneva Agreement to establish a large military advisory mission in Laos, so in 1958 a Program Evaluation Office (PEO) was established instead. The PEO was in fact a Central Intelligence Agency cover for a whole range of clandestine activities against the Pathet Lao and their North Vietnamese sponsors. The CIA began to recruit an army of Meo tribesmen, led by a Meo chief named Vang Pao who had fought for the French against the Viet Minh. By 1959 the CIA was using Meo guerrillas on intelligence gathering operations near the strategic Plain of Jars and in July 107 US Special Forces troops arrived to train Royal Lao Army Units and guerrilla groups in behind-the-lines warfare. Within a year the Special Forces 'White Star' teams and CIA officers had organized over 9000 Meo guerrillas, and soon they were blowing up communist supply dumps and harassing their logistics lines. Eventually the Meo army expanded to over 40,000 guerrillas and became the most effective irregular fighting force in Laos. In order to supply and provide transport for such a large force, the CIA's covert airline, Air America, gathered a huge fleet of aircraft together, including short take-off and landing (STOL) types such as the Helio Courier, PC-6 Pilatus Porter and Dornier DO-28, and transport aircraft like the C-7 Caribou,

BELOW: Air America's Helio Couriers were ideal for short rough airstrip work.
BOTTOM: USAF Skyraiders carrying bombs with long fuse extenders designed to detonate above the ground.

ABOVE: Air America Caribou, Helio Courier and British Royal Air Force Pioneer at Sam Thong airstrip in Laos.

C-46 Commando, C-47 Skytrain and C-123 Provider. Many of the transport types were provided direct from US military stocks and most were flown unmarked or wearing false markings.

The situation in Laos was further complicated by the traditional pattern of competition among a few ruling families and by 1960 a three-way civil war was underway between rightists, neutralists and the Pathet Lao. Events came to a head on 9 August when most members of the Royal Laotian government were in the royal capital of Luang Prabang, a hundred miles north of Vientiane, attending funeral ceremonies for King Sisavang Vong. Captain Kong Le, a paratrooper battalion commander, disgusted with the continuing civil war, used the opportunity to take control of Vientiane, dissolve the

right-wing cabinet of Prince Somsanith and invite Prince Souvanna Phouma to form a neutralist government.

When news of the coup reached Luang Prabang, General Phoumi Nosavan, a right-wing military leader who dominated the Sannikone government, flew to his home in Savannakhet. It was there, with most of the conservatives in the National Assembly that he established a 'Committee Against the Coup d'Etat'. The US government began backing the Savannakhet group with money and arms while maintaining formal diplomatic relations with the Vientiane government under the neutralist Souvanna Phouma. In late November General Nosavan's troops marched northward up National Route 13, reaching Vientiane in early December. A battle raged around the city for three days before Kong Le retreated northward to the Plain of Jars with the remnants of his followers.

In early December, Kong Le, already in a temporary alliance with the

Pathet Lao and North Vietnamese Army units operating in northeast Laos, began receiving arms and supplies from a Soviet airlift. On 16 December the American Air Attaché, Colonel Butler B Toland, Jr, photographed a Soviet Il-14 dropping supplies to the Kong Le forces near Vang Vieng. A few days later the Embassy's VC-47 Skytrain was on a reconnaissance flight over the Plain of Jars when it was fired upon by Kong Le and Pathet Lao troops, a 0.50-inch caliber machine gun bullet wounding the radio operator. This was the first US Air Force aircraft fired at by the communists in the Southeast Asia conflict.

In March 1961 President John F Kennedy announced to a press conference that the Russians had flown over 1000 supply flights into Laos for the Kong Le and Pathet Lao forces. On the 23rd of that month the first American aircraft was lost to enemy action.

A specially-modified intelligence-gathering SC-47 took off from Vien-

tiane and set a course for a Pathet Lao base which was on the eastern edge of the Plain of Jars, called Xieng Khouangville. Its mission was to determine the frequencies used by Soviet pilots to locate the airfield through the dense fog which often covered the area. Suddenly, shells from a Pathet Lao anti-aircraft gun slammed into the aircraft, shearing off a wing and sending the plane plummeting toward the jungle. A US Army major who always wore a parachute when he flew, jumped from the falling aircraft and was captured by the Pathet Lao. He spent 17 months as a prisoner before being repatriated after the signing of the Geneva Agreements on Laos in 1962.

President Kennedy did not want to commit American ground troops to combat in Laos, but was prepared to support the pro-western forces by covert means instead. Sixteen H-34 Choctaw helicopters were provided to Air America and these were flown by civilian crews. In addition, the survival of the neutralist government in Vientiane depended on the acquisition of useful intelligence about enemy activities, so the US covertly sent reconnaissance and combat aircraft to Thailand as the North Vietnamese moved more anti-aircraft units on to the Plain of Jars. The Royal Thai Air Force had been providing reconnaissance support to Laos with their Lockheed RT-33A Shooting Star jets, but in February 1961 they were withdrawn. President Kennedy was reluctant to authorize the use of US Air Force McDonnell RF-101 Voodoo jets, so some RT-33s were borrowed from the Philippine Air Force, painted with Laotian markings and flown on reconnaissance missions over Laos by Air Force pilots. The first of these sorties was flown from Udorn on 24 April 1961 under the code name *Field Goal*. Eight days earlier six North American F-100 Super Sabre fighters from the 510th Tactical Fighter Squadron at Clark Air Base in the Philippines had flown into Don Muang International Airport outside Bangkok, ostensibly to provide air defense, under the code name *Bell Tone*.

The United States and the Soviet Union realized that their two countries

18

ABOVE: A Royal Thai Air Force Lockheed T-33 at Don Muang airport in Thailand.

were on a possible collision course in Laos and arranged an international conference to work out a political solution to the Laotian problem. The Geneva Conference on Laos opened in May 1961, and lasted until July 1962 when the three Lao factions, Neutralists, Pathet Lao and Rightists, finally agreed on a delicate settlement. Prince Souvanna Phouma established a coalition which lasted from July 1962 until fighting resumed in April 1963.

The 1962 Geneva Agreement stipulated a deadline for the withdrawal of all foreign military elements. Inspectors from the International Control Commission checked and counted each military adviser as he left the country. There were 666 of them and by the deadline the only uniformed Americans or intelligence officers left in Laos were the Army and Air Force attachés and their staffs at the Embassy. The ICC could not check the communist foreign military out of the country, as they were not permitted to visit Pathet Lao territory. It was estimated that there were 10,000 regular soldiers from North Vietnam still in the country. Behind this phony neutrality which existed only in the world's newspapers and in diplomats' minds, the war continued.

The problem for the United States was how to appear to be keeping the Geneva Agreements and yet evade them at the same time. Military advisers and CIA personnel moved across the border into Thailand, where they were flown in every day by Air America, whose entire helicopter operation was based in Udorn. The CIA and General Vang Pao moved into a virtually uninhabited mountain bowl called Long Tieng and developed it into the largest Agency field headquarters in the world. Directed from this base, Vang Pao's guerrillas continued to fight against the Pathet Lao and the North Vietnamese troops protecting the Ho Chi Minh trail, but on the whole 1962 was relatively quiet. In the meantime the focus in the Southeast Asia conflict had shifted back to Vietnam.

2. Farm Gate to the Gulf of Tonkin

In 1960 the Central Committee of the Lao Dong Party, the Communist party of North Vietnam, passed a resolution that South Vietnam was to be 'liberated' and that North and South Vietnam were to be unified under a 'progressive socialist' administration. In December Hanoi radio announced the formation in South Vietnam of the National Front for the Liberation of South Vietnam, a front which Hanoi claimed was made up of several political parties of South Vietnamese. Subsequent broadcasts identified a 'People's Revolutionary Party' as the leading party in this so-called front. It is significant that no announcement of this came out of South Vietnam and no nationally-known South Vietnamese figure was ever identified with any of the political parties, which seemed to exist on paper only and in broadcasts by Hanoi radio.

The Viet Cong intensified its guerrilla war against President Ngo Dinh Diem's regime early in 1961. By March, US intelligence analysts estimated that the guerrillas were killing, assassinating or kidnapping 500 pro-government village officials, teachers and soldiers every month. Secretary of State Dean Rusk reported at a Washington press conference on 4 May that

the Viet Cong had grown in number to 12,000 and had killed or kidnapped more than 3000 persons in 1960.

In May 1961 President Kennedy sent Vice-President Lyndon B Johnson to South Vietnam to consult with President Diem. As a result of the discussions the United States agreed to increase its military aid to South Vietnam by funding the expansion of the South Vietnamese Army from 170,000 to 200,000 men and providing the Vietnamese Air Force (VNAF) with a second fighter squadron. The squadron was to be made up of North American T-28 Trojans, taken out of storage in America and modified as T-28Ds. It was felt that because of its robust construction and ability to withstand hard landings, the T-28 would be very suitable in the counter-insurgency role. A third liaison squadron equipped with 0-1 Bird Dogs would be formed and eventually a photographic reconnaissance unit would also be provided. Additional training centers would be set up, including an American/South Vietnamese combat development and test center which would learn and improve counter-insurgency techniques and tactics. One of their ideas soon to be put into practice was the use of aerial-delivered defoliants to reduce jungle

cover along major highways, where the Viet Cong frequently ambushed government convoys.

At this time the United States Armed Forces had little knowledge or expertise in the art of counter-insurgency warfare. This applied particularly to the Air Force which was organized and equipped to fight a war in a modern nuclear conflict setting, rather than against guerrilla units on a battlefield consisting mainly of jungle and mountains. President Kennedy ordered that new units be formed to deal with this type of conflict and the Air Force responded by establishing the 4400th Combat Crew Training Squadron (CCTS) at Eglin Air Force Base in Florida on 14 April 1961. The squadron was code named *Jungle Jim* and its mission was to specialize in counter-insurgency tactics, using aircraft more suitable to the conditions prevailing in countries like Vietnam.

In September 1961 Viet Cong attacks increased sharply and there were indications of some weakening in Diem's

---

PAGES 20-21: Its fuselage blackened by exhaust smoke, a USAF Skyraider after a mission.
BELOW: Troops deploy from a Marine Corps Sikorsky H-34 helicopter.

military position. At the end of the month Diem requested a treaty that would commit the United States to defend South Vietnam. In response President Kennedy sent his chief military adviser General Maxwell D Taylor, US Army, and Dr Walt Rostow to South Vietnam to survey the situation. The news was not good. It was General Taylor's view that South Vietnam was in trouble and major US interests were at stake. He argued that the communist strategy of taking over Southeast Asia by guerrilla warfare was well on its way to success in South Vietnam, aided by the unpopular and inefficient government of President Diem. As a result of General Taylor's recommendations President Kennedy approved a more active program of support to South Vietnam including the establishment of a joint headquarters for directing the program; increasing the number of US advisers for the South Vietnamese forces, and additional deployment of Army Aviation and Air Force units.

On 10 November 1961 Detachment

RIGHT: A UH-1A of the UTTHCO on field trials prior to deployment to Vietnam.
BELOW: US Army H-21 Shawnees flare over a landing zone near Ap Loi An in April 1963.

2A of the 4400th CCTS, designated *Farm Gate*, left Eglin for Vietnam. They took with them four SC-47 Skytrains, eight T-28s and four Douglas B-26 bombers, although the latter were listed as RB-26 reconnaissance aircraft, rather than bombers, to stay in line with the Geneva Agreement which forbade the introduction of bombers into Indochina. Significantly all the aircraft carried Vietnamese Air Force markings. By the end of December the *Farm Gate* aircraft and personnel were established at Bien Hoa Air Base and operations soon began. One of the detachment's first tasks was to get the Vietnamese T-28s operational and extensive instruction in flight training, gunnery, bombing and rocketry enabled the T-28 squadron to become operational in March 1962. In order to increase the number of operational T-28s, 30 US pilots were assigned to the two VNAF C-47 squadrons, thus releasing the C-47 pilots for assignment to a second T-28 squadron. The US pilots, nicknamed the *Dirty Thirty*, served as co-pilots with the Vietnamese crews until the unit disbanded in December 1963.

This combined unit was under the leadership of Nguyen Cao Ky, who was to become the chief of the Vietnamese Air Force and a future Prime Minister.

Meanwhile, toward the end of the year, communist Pathet Lao forces accelerated their operations against the Royal Government of Laos. At the same time several Viet Cong units of up to 1500 men began cutting strategic highways in the vicinity of Saigon and other urban areas. This notable rise in insurgent activities led President Diem to proclaim a state of emergency. USAF advisers asked for the deployment of a detachment of four RF-101 Voodoos to Tan Son Nhut to conduct reconnaissance missions over Vietnam and Laos.

An invitation from the VNAF for the USAF to take part in an air show in October 1961 provided the excuse to send jets into the area. On the 18th, four RF-101Cs from the 15th Tactical Reconnaissance Squadron (TRS) deployed to Saigon International Airport under the code name *Pipe Stem* task force. Over the following 31 days they flew 67 sorties over the Laotian Plain of Jars and parts of the Ho Chi Minh trail

until they were withdrawn following North Vietnamese complaints to the International Control Commission. In order to supplement and eventually replace the Tan Son Nhut detachment the Royal Thai government agreed to let USAF RF-101s operate out of Don Muang airport and on 7 November the *Able Mabel* task force became operational when four RF-101Cs of the 45th TRS arrived from Japan. By the end of the year they had flown 130 missions.

One of the problem areas highlighted by General Taylor's visit to Vietnam was the lack of mobility of Army of the Republic of Vietnam (ARVN) troops. The inadequate road networks and geographical conditions often hindered the movement of troops by vehicle and there were not enough helicopters to go around. President Kennedy decided to send a USAF squadron of 16 Fairchild C-123B Provider tactical assault transport aircraft under the code name *Mule Train* and these began to arrive at Tan

BELOW: A *Farm Gate* B-26 armed with four napalm bombs and two rocket pods.

ABOVE: Vietnamese troops and American advisers unload a Marine H-34 under fire.

Son Nhut in December. The Provider was actually scheduled to be phased out of the Air Force inventory in 1961, but when Secretary of Defense Robert S McNamara suggested that the Air Force turn over the C-123s to the Army to train on the type prior to the receipt of the C-7 Caribou, the Air Force suddenly discovered new and pressing requirements for the C-123. Although the twin engined transport could carry a healthy load of cargo, its gross weight of 55,700 pounds meant that it could only operate into 11 percent of the airfields in South Vietnam.

Apart from the transport aircraft, President Kennedy also ordered the deployment of US Army helicopter units to Vietnam and on 11 December

the USS *Card* sailed into Saigon with the Piasecki CH-21C Shawnees of the 8th and 57th Transportation Companies (Light Helicopter) on board. The Shawnee, nicknamed the *Flying Banana* was a single-engined, twin-rotor helicopter which had been developed in the late 1950s. It was rather underpowered and slow, but under the circumstances anything was better than nothing and soon the helicopters were on their way to Tan Son Nhut airport where they were prepared for operations as the first major American unit in Vietnam.

On 15 November 1961 Detachment 7 of the 13th Air Force was established at Tan Son Nhut. Five days later Brigadier General Rollen H Anthis, Vice Commander of the 13th Air Force, became Commander, Detachment 7, 2nd ADVON (Advanced Echelon). On 1 December he was named Chief, Air

Force Section, Military Assistance Advisory Group, Vietnam.

In January 1962 the US Air Force began to assist the Vietnamese in setting up a Tactical Air Control System (TACS), which is essential to the proper employment of airpower within a theater of operations. Although the VNAF was nominally responsible for the system, the USAF in fact operated the TACS from the outset. There was initially opposition to the idea of centralized control of air assets from the four Vietnamese Corps Commanders who preferred to have the final say on how the air effort would be used in their areas. However, a Control and Reporting Center (CRC), the main block of the system with the heaviest radars, was installed at Tan Son Nhut. A Control and Reporting Post (CRP) was then established at Da Nang, followed by a Vietnamese-operated radar CRP at

Pleiku. This radar network, which provided limited aircraft control and warning coverage over all of South Vietnam, soon began picking up tracks of numerous unidentified aircraft. Ironically, the TACS was first tested operationally on 27 February 1962 when two disaffected VNAF pilots strafed and bombed the presidential palace in Saigon. One of the A-1 Skyraiders was shot down and the other escaped to Cambodia. The creation of a Tactical Air Control Center (TACC) was to follow later, but at that time an Air Operations Center (AOC) functioned as a TACC.

Whereas the TACS is concerned with the physical control of aircraft and seeing that the aircraft carry out the assigned mission, the air-ground operations system is the heart of the decision process in determining what, where and when those aircraft will strike. It is the air-ground operations system that can make or break close air support effectiveness.

Prior to the introduction of US units in 1961, there was a very rudimentary air-ground operations system between the ARVN and VNAF. There was no overall commander of combat operations or what can be considered a theater commander. General Cao Van Vien, Chief of the General Staff, came closest to being an overall commander, but the normal arrangement was to make the four Corps Commanders almost autonomous. Each Corps covered a different part of South Vietnam; I Corps covered the northern part of the country adjacent to the DMZ, II Corps the Central Highlands, III Corps the area surrounding Saigon and IV Corps the southern delta. The Corps Commanders reported directly to the President on all civil matters in the area and received directions from the President on critical military matters, although they were technically responsible to the Chief of the General Staff. This arrangement made the Joint General Staff relatively weak and as a result, the JGS could not co-ordinate the activities of the Corps as closely as needed, particularly where priority for use of air assets was an issue.

TOP: A VNAF Cessna O-1 Bird Dog spotter plane at Tan Son Nhut Air Base.
MIDDLE: The Bird Dog was also used by the Marine Observation Squadrons.
LEFT: The U-1 Otter was flown by the US Army Transportation units.

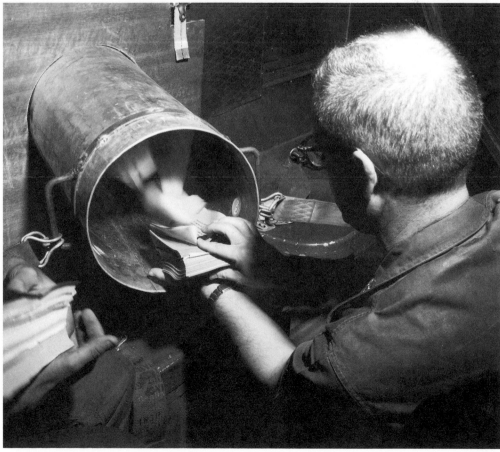

ABOVE: Secretary of Defense McNamara (right) and General Lemnitzer, Chairman of the JCS.
RIGHT: Propaganda leaflets in the dispersal chute of a Psy-war C-47.

With American aircraft and helicopters being introduced to the theater of operations a change in the slow and inadequate air-ground operations system was needed to conform with accepted USAF doctrine. Initially Air Support Operations Centers (ASOCs), later redesignated Direct Air Support Centers (DASCs) were established at each of the Corps' headquarters. These were manned by VNAF and USAF personnel. The ASOCs were located within a short distance of the Corps' Tactical Operations Center (TOC). The procedure was that a request for air support would go from the Division to the Corps TOC where it was coordinated with the ASOC. The ASOC would then process the request to the Air Operations Center and if the AOC could satisfy it, execute the mission. If it was beyond their capabilities, it would

go to the Joint Operations Center, the operational element of the Joint General Staff in Saigon, for a decision as to which Corps would get the mission. This was the path a pre-planned request followed. If an urgent request developed (an immediate), aircraft were diverted from a pre-planned target. This was the procedure until the deployment of major US forces in 1964.

As the deployment of the Tactical Air Control System began on 1 January 1962 under the nickname *Barn Door*, the newly-arrived Shawnees were preparing to go into action. Within a fortnight of arriving in Vietnam, the 8th and 57th Transportation Companies carried out Operation *Chopper*, the first major airlift action of the war. Over one thousand ARVN paratroopers and their American advisers were airlifted into a Viet Cong base complex a mere 10 miles west of Saigon. The Viet Cong were surprised by this first large scale

use of helicopters and offered little resistance, melting away into the surrounding jungle and leaving behind a quantity of supplies and a transmitter which had been used to broadcast anti-government propaganda. A number of problems had shown up during the operation though, including poor air-ground communications and embarkation and disembarkation difficulties experienced by the small ARVN troops who found it hard to climb aboard and jump out of the H-21s with full packs and equipment.

The first few helicopters to arrive in country were based at Tan Son Nhut and provided support to all the ARVN units they could reach. Naturally, this support was based on operational priorities and the average ARVN infantry unit saw very few helicopters in its day to day operations. This was, however, a period of innovation and of trial and error schooling for the US

ABOVE: H-21s approach a landing zone.
ABOVE RIGHT: An HH-43 with a fire suppression bottle hovers over a crashed A-1 at Da Nang.
RIGHT: The HH-43B Huskie was a short range rescue helicopter.

pilots and crews, and also for the Viet Cong.

There is one hair-raising tale of the H-21 pilot who put down in a landing zone only to see a squad of Viet Cong step from the woods and open fire on him at point blank range. Fortunately for the pilot and crew, the Viet Cong squad leader had firmly embedded in the minds of his men the necessity to lead the helicopter with their fire. The amazed pilot watched the squad pour their fire into the ground 20 yards in front of him. He took off without a single hit. This kind of strange tale in a sense characterizes the early days of air mobility in the Vietnam war.

Soon the two H-21 companies found themselves extremely overworked and, in January 1962, the 93rd Transportation Company was sent on board the USS *Card* to join them. Their H-21s were prepared for flight aboard the ship and they flew straight off the flight deck of the *Card* to Da Nang, 10 miles away, despite ceilings down to 100 feet over the ocean.

Although there were now three helicopter companies in the country; two at Tan Son Nhut and one at Da Nang, they were hard pressed due to a critical shortage of engines. Deterioration of rotor blades and aviation equipment due to the high humidity also added to the problem. In order to establish a utility supply network for the H-21s the 18th Aviation Company was sent out from Fort Riley, Kansas, with their U-1A Otter aircraft and they were soon flying parts and supplies the length and breadth of the country.

In order to provide better command and control of the Army's growing fleet, the 45th Transportation Battalion was deployed to Vietnam in early 1962 from Fort Sill, Oklahoma, and assumed command of the three helicopter companies and the fixed-wing Otter company. Shortly thereafter two more light helicopter companies, the 33rd and the 81st, were deployed and they also came under the command of the 45th Transportation Battalion. By June the five H-21 units were deployed throughout the four military regions into which South Vietnam had been divided.

At 1630 hours on 7 January 1962

ABOVE AND RIGHT: *Ranch Hand* C-123 Providers on defoliation missions. Over nineteen million gallons of herbicides were sprayed over South Vietnam including eleven million of *Agent Orange*.

three C-123 Providers landed at Tan Son Nhut Air Base and taxied to a secure fenced area on the field, sharing the space normally occupied by President Diem's personal aircraft. They had come from Clark Air Base in the Philippines where they and three others had spent the previous month, waiting for Presidential clearance to proceed to Vietnam. These were no ordinary Providers for they had aluminum alloy armor plating under and around the cockpit and were fitted with the MC-1 *Hourglass* spray system complete with 1000 gallon spray tank and underwing nozzles. They had arrived to begin Operation *Ranch Hand*, a program designed to defoliate areas of the countryside to deny cover to the Viet Cong and to kill crops to deny them food. The idea had originated at the Combat Development and Test Center and had four objectives; firstly, to strip the Cambodian-Laotian-North Vietnamese border of foliage to remove the protective cover from Viet Cong reinforcements, secondly to defoliate a portion of the Mekong Delta area known as *War Zone D*, in which the Viet Cong had many bases, thirdly, to destroy numerous abandoned manioc groves which the Viet Cong used as food sources and fourthly, to destroy mangrove swamps within which the

Viet Cong took refuge. Unfortunately the program would have meant the defoliation of over 31,000 square miles of jungle, an area equivalent to about half of South Vietnam. This ambitious plan was soon dropped in favor of a more limited scheme.

The debate raged in government circles for some time as to whether or not the program was to be overt or covert in view of the possibility of communist claims of chemical warfare. Ambassador Nolting in Saigon recommended that the aircraft carry civilian markings and their crews wear civilian clothes, but in the end the decision was made not to disguise the identity of the aircraft or their crews. While the decision was being taken the USAF flew

RIGHT: The HU-16 Albatross saved forty-seven aircrew while deployed in Southeast Asia.

some 35,000 pounds of herbicides into Vietnam, bypassing International Control Commission inspection. Soon afterwards the US Department of Defense announced that in view of the acts of aggression being carried out by North Vietnam, in flagrant violation of the Geneva Accords, the United States would no longer announce the arrival of personnel and equipment to the ICC. By the first week of January 208,000 gallons of chemicals were aboard two cargo ships, destination Vietnam.

The first test flight took place on 10 January 1962 and formal operations commenced three days later. The aircraft were flown by USAF pilots with a Vietnamese 'aircraft commander' who had no actual authority over the mission and was there merely to give the impression that it was a Vietnamese operation. In fact, on one occasion when an American pilot persuaded his Vietnamese 'aircraft commander' to take over the controls his erratic handling soon convinced the crew that he was not a pilot, and they subsequently learned that the VNAF had been sending them navigators, and

later they were sent anyone who happened to be available, whether officer or enlisted.

The defoliation operations were not without cost however, because on 2 February a *Ranch Hand* C-123 crashed, killing the crew of three. These were the first Air Force fatalities in Vietnam. The aircraft crashed in an inaccessible area and it took some time for a search party to arrive, escorted by a company of ARVN troops. They found no evidence of sabotage, engine failure or hits by ground fire, and the cause of the crash was never officially determined. Shortly afterward however, the 13th Air Force, which had recently established a detachment at Tan Son Nhut, requested fighter escorts for all future *Ranch Hand* operations. Nine days later the first *Farm Gate* aircraft was lost when an SC-47A on a leaflet-dropping mission crashed in the mountains 70 miles northeast of Saigon. Secretary of Defense Robert McNamara subsequently criticized the mission and re-emphasized that American forces were supposed to be training the Vietnamese and not

to be undertaking combat activities.

The defoliation flights continued until 20 March when they were suspended for five months while the whole program was re-evaluated. Many complaints had been made by villagers of damage caused to their trees and crops by the defoliant, which often spread over a greater area than planned. This was used to full advantage by Viet Cong propagandists.

Four of the original six *Ranch Hand* C-123s were later converted back to the tactical airlift role and near the end of April one of these crashed while on a cargo mission. The aircraft was operating in the north of the country and was landing at an airstrip when, to the pilot's surprise, Vietnamese came running towards his aircraft. The pilot

---

BELOW: Two VNAF T-28s on a counter-insurgency training mission.
RIGHT: An A-1 Skyraider from the VNAF's 522nd Squadron taxies out at Tan Son Nhut.
BOTTOM RIGHT: A VNAF single-seater A-1H Skyraider armed with bombs and napalm.

LEFT: The Grumman OV-1B Mohawk carried side-looking airborne radar.
BOTTOM LEFT: The OV-1A was fitted with a panoramic camera for horizon-to-horizon coverage.

On 13 January 1962, the day that *Ranch Hand* missions began, T-28 Trojans from the 4400th Combat Crew Training Squadron's *Farm Gate* detachment at Bien Hoa, flew their first Vietnamese Forward Air Controller (FAC) directed mission against Viet Cong besieging an ARVN outpost. The Forward Air Controllers in their Cessna 0-1 Bird Dogs and the Air Liaison Officers on the ground were the last elements in the air-ground operations system. The FAC would ensure that the ground-attack aircraft delivered their ordnance in the right place, usually marking the target area themselves with rockets mounted under their wings.

Although the *Farm Gate* aircraft were officially there in the combat training role, they were authorized to 'fire back if fired upon.' This was then extended to undertaking actual combat operations, but only when a VNAF crewman was aboard or when the VNAF lacked the ability to perform certain missions. These early rules of engagement grew longer and more detailed in the years that followed, telling pilots what they could or could not do in combat. The President of the United States and his advisers retained tight control over the air operations throughout much of the war, with the initial intention of avoiding the military intervention of Russia or China. Events were to show that the restrictions and controls imposed by inexperienced civilians thousands of miles away from the action, often adversely affected operations; caused the lives of pilots to be lost unnecessarily and contributed in no small part to the eventual failure of the United States to defeat the North Vietnamese.

On 29 January *Farm Gate* T-28s and B-26 bombers attacked targets from Saigon to as far north as Quang Tri Province, near the Demilitarized Zone. During the month the crews flew 229 sorties, together with various leaflet drops, psychological warfare broadcasts and flare-drop missions performed by their SC-47s. The *Night Angel* flare-drop missions were the salvation of many outposts and strategic hamlets in the strife-torn countryside. Usually the Viet Cong would attack

thought he had landed in North Vietnam by mistake and attempted to take off again. As he opened the throttles he found that he did not have enough height to clear a railway embankment and reversed the maneuver to drop down on the ground again. The impact buckled the floor and irreparably damaged the aircraft, although the wings and engines were salvaged.

Ranch Hand C-123s resumed spraying operations in September 1962 and over the next ten years over 19 million gallons of herbicides would be sprayed over South Vietnam. Eleven million gallons were of the type known as *Agent Orange*, as identified by the colored bands around the drums. It consisted of a mixture of chemicals (2,4 dichloro-phen-oxyacetic acid and 2,4,5 trichloro-phenoxyacetic acid). The defoliation program was halted in 1971 following the banning of the chemicals in the United States because of concern about the possible effects of the chemicals on humans. By the end of the program 41 percent of the mangrove forests in South Vietnam had been affected, together with 19 percent of the uplands forests and 8 percent of all cultivated land. Despite the best intentions of the USAF *Agent Orange* was sprayed not only over the countryside, but over the soldiers and civilian population as well. At the time of writing over 16,000 veterans had filed disability claims against the US Government for health damage allegedly due to *Agent Orange*.

under the cover of darkness and especially during the period just before daylight. To counter this, C-47 flare ships would fly an all-night vigil over certain portions of the country, ready to heed the call of a besieged outpost with an umbrella of light. Often just the brilliant illumination produced by the paraflares would be enough to cause the Viet Cong to break off their attack, rather than wait around for an airstrike to arrive. The VNAF began to increase its number of sorties by flying both day and night and in January its single squadron of 22 A-1H Skyraiders flew 251 combat sorties. One area in which the VNAF began to prove its mettle was in convoy and train escort. Between January and July 1962 these sorties totalled slightly over 100, but by fall that year the figure was nearly 200 a month. Losses from Viet Cong ambushes declined sharply when the VNAF began to put an 0-1 Bird Dog FAC and a flight of strike aircraft above each important convoy. A similar result was achieved when strike aircraft began escorting both passenger and freight trains along those portions of the railroad where communist attacks were most frequent.

In February 1962 the Kennedy administration established the US Military Assistance Command, Vietnam (USMACV) as an umbrella agency to co-ordinate US military policy, assistance and operations in South Vietnam. General Paul D Harkins, US Army, was appointed its commander. He also assumed command of the US Military Assistance Command, Thailand (USMAC THAI) when it was established on 15 May, following President Kennedy's announcement of his intention to deploy US forces to that country.

A pacification program began in March to counter Viet Cong influence in the countryside and expand government control over villages where the Viet Cong might find support. The program was based on the recommendations of Sir Robert Thompson, head of the British Advisory Mission in Saigon from 1961-65. The idea was similar to that used by the British when dealing with Chinese terrorists in Malaya between 1949-59. The plan was to resettle villagers in fortified strategic hamlets in relatively safe 'white' areas, thus depriving the Viet Cong of supplies and local recruits. From there ARVN troops would move farther and farther into Viet Cong 'red' areas, 'like a

slowly spreading oil spot,' and eventually drive the insurgents out of the country.

On 16 March, in a much publicized start of the Strategic Hamlet Program, the ARVN 5th Division launched Operation *Sunrise*. It began with a motorized deployment of ARVN troops to the southern fringes of the Viet Cong's Zone D sanctuary in Binh Duong province. Once there the soldiers moved out to uproot the peasants, believed to be supplying the insurgents with food, and relocate them elsewhere in fortified hamlets which they were compelled to build themselves. Following the success of this initial operation, President Diem ordered a rapid expansion of the Strategic Hamlet Program. The President's brother, Ngo Dinh

Nhu, was responsible for the program, but it was doomed to failure for a number of reasons. There was no strategic direction and hamlets were scattered without mutual support. Military operations were not designed to support the program and not enough effort was made to weed out the Viet Cong and their supporters from inside the hamlets. The program also went too fast, with 8000 fortified hamlets being created within two years, whereas in Malaya it had taken three years to organize just 500. President Diem's death in 1963 and subsequent coups put an end to the program and eventually

BELOW: Bombs exploding on Viet Cong structures along a canal.

the Viet Cong won back control of the countryside.

Unidentified radar tracks over South Vietnam on 19 and 20 March 1962 prompted the Commander-in-Chief Pacific (CINCPAC) to direct the deployment of four Convair F-102 Delta Dagger interceptors to Tan Son Nhut on the 21st. One week later they returned to Clark Air Base without making any active intercepts. Additional *Water Glass* deployments continued throughout the year, using two-seat TF-102As which were more effective against the low-slow targets.

The US Army and Air Force both had squadrons operational in Vietnam; now it was the turn of the Marine Corps. In March 1962 they were ordered to deploy a helicopter squadron to Vietnam and planning began for Operation *Shufly*. On 8 April Colonel John F Carey, the Chief of Staff of the 1st Marine Air Wing, and his staff arrived at Cubi Point Naval Air Station in the Philippines in a Douglas C-117, en route to Vietnam. The next morning

they discovered that the aircraft had developed mechanical difficulties and could not proceed. Colonel Carey was remembered as surveying the aircraft and exploding 'We have a war going on and now our horse just died!' There was, fortunately, another C-117 at Cubi on a routine logistics flight for the 1st MAW. Colonel Carey walked over to the pilot, a captain, and said 'Too bad your airplane is sick.' The captain responded that his aircraft was in fine shape. 'Oh no it isn't' Colonel Carey answered. 'Yours is over there and it's sick. This one is mine.' By the afternoon of 9 April the advance party had arrived at Soc Trang in South Vietnam. The airfield was 85 miles southwest of Saigon in the Mekong Delta. It had been built by the Japanese during World War II and had a 3000 feet long concrete runway, a distinct bonus in the Delta where most roads and runways were surfaced with laterite, a red clay, which when dry has the consistency of talcum powder and when wet, bottomless glue.

Other airfield facilities were nonexistent, however, so the C-117 pilot converted his aircraft into an improvized control tower. He removed the escape hatch on top of the cockpit, turned on the radios, put his sun glasses on, stuck his head out and said 'Hallo there, this is Soc Trang tower.' He then gave landing instructions to the KC-130 Hercules transports bringing fuel, water and supplies into the airfield. Six days later Marine Helicopter Squadron HMM-362 flew its 24 Sikorsky UH-34D Seahorses off the USS *Princeton* and into Soc Trang. They were accompanied by a C-117 for transport and liaison and three 0-1B Bird Dogs from Marine Squadron VMO-2.

Within ten days one of the H-34's had been shot down by a single bullet which pierced an oil pipe in the engine and highlighted the need for armor plating

BELOW: An RF-101 Voodoo reconnaissance jet photographs its own shadow while flying over an NVA 57mm anti-aircraft gun site.

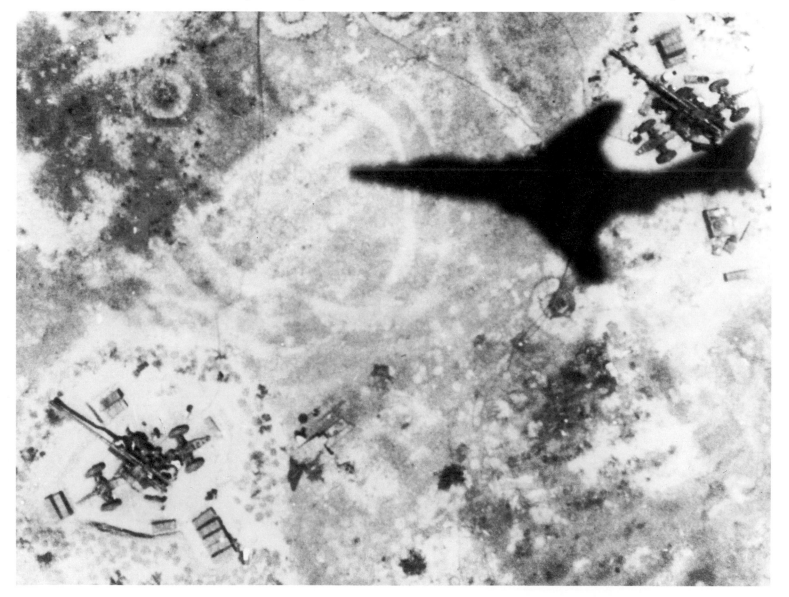

ABOVE: The first McDonnell RF-101 Voodoos arrived in Southeast Asia in 1961.

around such vulnerable areas. The squadron swapped bases in June with the 93rd Aviation Company at Da Nang, because the H-34s were more capable of operating in the high elevations of the northern portion of the country than the underpowered H-21s, which were also only marginally suited for night and instrument flying.

By the time HMM-362 was relieved in August it had identified almost every area which would eventually require further development in helicopters. Armor plating was needed, as was some form of firepower to help suppress enemy fire when close to or on the ground. Landing in the face of heavy fire, particularly from machine guns, was 'foolhardy,' and new body armor and flight clothing for crews was given a high priority. Also urgently needed was an armed escort for the troop-carrying helicopters, to attack immediately any enemy around the landing zone. In this particular field the Army was way ahead.

The Army's H-21s had started to receive ground fire when flying into and out of landing zones. The crew chiefs responded by returning fire with infantry weapons and then mounting 0.30-inch Browning machine guns in the open doorways. Even if the disadvantage of partially blocking the doorways was discounted this suppressive fire was not enough and fixed-wing aircraft were not always available for escort duties. It soon became evident that the solution to the problem might be in the employment of armed gunship helicopters.

The 53rd Aviation Detachment on Okinawa had been operating 15 Bell UH-1A Iroquois as part of the Aviation Support Activity on the island. In July 1962 these 'Hueys' (from the original designation HU-1A) were used to form the Utility Tactical Transport Helicopter Company (UTTHCO) and under the guidance of Warrant Officer Cletus Heck the UH-1As were fitted with a locally fabricated weapons system. This initial armament consisted of two fixed forward-firing 0.30-inch machine guns and 16 2.75-inch folding-fin aerial rockets, procured from the Air Force. A single machine gun was fitted to each landing skid and fed from ammunition boxes inside the cargo compartment, while eight launch tubes for the rockets were fixed to the rear of each skid.

The three platoons of UH-1As arrived at Tan Son Nhut Air Base on 25 July and flew their first escort mission for the H-21s nine days later. The UTTHCO was under the direct operational control of USMACV and its effectiveness was studied by an Army Concept Team of evaluators during a test period from October 1962 to March 1963. The test plan called for the evaluation of the UH-1A armed helicopter in the escort role. Although this was not defined, actual experience determined that the escort role broke down into an 'en route phase,' that was usually flown at a safe height; an 'approach phase' where the heliborne force usually descended to nap-of-the-earth heights several kilometers away from the landing zone, and the 'landing zone phase.' It was in the last phase that the armed helicopters proved most valuable, suppressing enemy ground fire. The tests proved that the suppressive fire delivered by the armed helicopters was highly effective in reducing the amount and accuracy of enemy fire against the transport helicopters. The gunships were here to stay.

The UH-1As had to be fitted with jury-rigged systems as the model lacked the built-in provisions for armament, such as external hard point mounts, electrical wiring and hydraulic piping. It also lacked power reserves when used in the hot and humid climate of Vietnam. Consequently a UH-1B model was produced which took advantage of the increased power available in the improved T53-L-5 engine. This replaced the original L-1 engine and was in turn replaced by the L-9 which gave even better performance. The first eleven much-improved UH-1Bs were shipped to the UTTHCO in Vietnam in October 1962, armed with the XM-6 Emerson 'Quad Gun' system. The quad guns, or flex guns as they became known, were a vast improvement over the UH-1As fixed guns. The quad guns on their hydraulic turrets were controlled by the co-pilot via a flexible pantographic sight mounted on the cabin roof. The guns could be depressed 85 degrees and elevated 10 degrees and moved sideways 10 degrees inboard and 70 degrees outward. The guns were fed by a dozen 500-round ammunition boxes mounted on the rear cabin floor. The linked rounds were fed through flexible metal chuting, assisted by electric drive motors on the turret casings. The advantage of the new 'flex guns' was that they could be fired at targets independent of the helicopter's flight path. With the two door gunners each armed with a standard M-60 machine gun and the jury-rigged rocket system developed for the A model, the UH-1B became a formidable fire support platform.

While the US Army was concentrat-

ing on the transportation of ARVN troops in the H-21s and the development of UH-1 escort gunships, other aviation units began to arrive in-country. Following a request from US advisers for a medical evacuation capability, the 57th Medical Detachment (Helicopter Ambulance) was deployed to Nha Trang and Qui Nhon. Their five UH-1As arrived on 2 May 1962, a full two months ahead of the UTTHCO and were the first of the thousands of new Bell helicopters to serve in Vietnam.

By this time the first USAF losses had occurred and before the end of the year a total of six aircraft would be lost to enemy action. In response to the increasing pace of air activity Detachment 3, Pacific Air Rescue Center was established at Tan Son Nhut on 1 April 1962. The unit consisted of only three officers and two noncommissioned officers and was without any search and rescue aircraft. These were not forthcoming because of the official government position, that as the Air Force was not supposed to be undertaking combat operations, a search and rescue force could not be justified.

On 23 May the 73rd Aviation Company arrived in Saigon with its two-seater 0-1F Bird Dogs. Soon the 32 aircraft were spread in 15 separate locations all the way from Hue in the north to Bac Lieu in the south. Their main role was reconnaissance for the advisers, but they were also used for artillery adjustment, target acquisition, command and control, message pick-up, medical evacuation and radio relay. Over the following 14 months they were to record over 41,000 hours of flying time.

A second C-123 transport squadron, the 777th Tactical Control Squadron, arrived at Da Nang Air Base in June under the code name *Saw Buck II*. Their 16 aircraft joined those of the 346th TCS (code name *Mule Train*) flying daily missions as a part of the Southeast Asia Airlift System. The C-123s were limited in the number of airstrips from which they could operate, because of their weight and performance. The deployment of the Army's 1st Aviation Company to Southeast Asia on 23 July 1962 went a long way to improve the tactical airlift system. Initially their De Havilland C-7 Caribou aircraft were based in Thailand, but in December they redeployed to Vung Tau in South Vietnam where they were joined in July 1963 by the C-7s of the 61st Aviation Company.

The Caribou was designed to operate from short, rough airstrips and was an ideal aircraft for counter-insurgency work. It could clear a 50 foot barrier after a takeoff run of 1185 feet or land over the same obstacle within a distance of 1235 feet. An experimental YC-7 Caribou had arrived in Vietnam in August 1961 for testing under the auspices of the Advanced Research Projects Agency. Even the old Southeast Asia hands of Air America were impressed when the Caribou made its unbelievably slow, steep approach to some of the primitive airstrips.

LEFT: A Vought RF-8G Crusader about to launch from the *Coral Sea*.

Whereas the Provider was limited to 11 percent of the airfields, the Caribou could fly into 77 percent of all airstrips in South Vietnam.

After a storm of controversy in the Pentagon, the Army deployed the six Grumman OV-1 Mohawk aircraft of the 23rd Special Warfare Aviation Detachment to Vietnam in September 1962, for the purpose of providing air surveillance in support of ARVN forces. The Mohawks were initially based at Nha Trang, supporting the ARVN 9th Division and the Railway Security Agency. Visual and photographic reconnaissance by this twin-turbine aircraft produced a wealth of intelligence for the units they supported. Hundreds of structures, most of them camouflaged, were detected in Viet Cong base areas. At the same time, hundreds of people were sighted in suspect areas, and because of the detailed familiarity of Mohawk crews with the local situation and activity patterns, some of the people sighted could be positively identified as insurgents. One of the unique advantages of the Mohawk in reconnaissance was its noise to speed relationship, which allowed the aircraft to get within observation distance of people on the ground without alerting them to its presence.

When the Mohawks deployed to Vietnam their rules of employment specified that; on all operational flights a Vietnamese observer would be on board; that the aircraft would be armed with 0.5-inch machine guns only and that this armament would be used only when required to defend against a hostile attack. Although there was no standard armament for the OV-1s, various weapons were eventually carried, including rockets and napalm. Between 16 October 1962 and 15 March 1963 the 23rd Special Warfare Aviation Detachment flew more than 2000 hours in the performance of 785 combat support missions. It had delivered defensive fire 27 times, and had lost two aircraft. The cause of the loss of these two aircraft was never determined.

By the end of 1962 almost 4000 Viet Cong had been killed or wounded and Vietnamese Air Force aircraft had damaged or destroyed more than 11,500 structures belonging to the insurgents. They had also sunk over 1500 boats, a significant accomplishment in the Mekong Delta region of Vietnam where boats represent virtually the only means of transport in an area that has few roads, even fewer bridges and literally thousands of canals and other waterways. Against these figures the VNAF and US Army helicopters had begun to suffer their first losses, as had the *Farm Gate* and other USAF aircraft. Viet Cong anti-aircraft fire, particularly below 1000 feet, became more effective as they received more Soviet or Chinese-made 12.7mm heavy machine guns and by the end of 1962 the USAF had lost half a dozen aircraft to enemy ground fire.

On 31 December 1962, President Kennedy authorized an increase in the strength of the *Farm Gate* detachment and five T-28s, ten B-26s and two C-47s were despatched. At that time there were 11,300 US military advisers in South Vietnam and the strength of the South Vietnamese armed forces stood at 243,000 men.

On 2 January 1963 the ARVN 7th

BELOW: A US Army C-7 Caribou short take off and landing aircraft at Saigon.

ABOVE: Unidentified radar tracks over South Vietnam led to *Water Glass* F-102 interceptor deployments from March 1962.

Division suffered a major defeat in an operation to seize a Viet Cong radio transmitter near the village of Ap Bac, 15 miles northwest of My Tho in the Plain of Reeds. The division commander believed that the transmitter was guarded by only a company of Viet Cong and allowed the operation to go ahead, even though there was no tactical air support available. The village was in fact defended by 400 men of the 514th Viet Cong (Regular) Battalion, equipped with automatic rifles and

several heavy machine guns. As the heliborne force flared over the landing zone the Viet Cong opened fire, and within minutes five helicopters were destroyed and nine damaged.

The Air Operations Center diverted two A-1 Skyraiders to the scene, but artillery firing through the air space forced the aircraft to delay their attack. To add to the confusion Vietnamese Forward Air Controllers were unable to direct air strikes with any accuracy. The American advisers had extreme difficulty persuading the ARVN troops to advance and the enemy was allowed to withdraw under the cover of darkness, but not before a VNAF air strike had accidentally hit a friendly unit, causing

numerous casualties. As the Viet Cong began to withdraw the ARVN IV Corps Commander ordered three companies of Vietnamese paratroopers to be dropped by C-123s. He directed them to be dropped to the west of Ap Bac, although the enemy were withdrawing to the east and the confused ARVN troops spent the night engaging each other in fire fights while the enemy escaped. By the morning friendly casualties stood at 65 ARVN troops and three American advisers killed and 100 ARVN and six American advisers wounded. MACV was subsequently criticized for having allowed the operation to proceed without adequate fixed-wing air support. According to the Viet

41

Cong, the victory boosted their flagging morale and was a major turning point in their war effort.

On 9 March 1963 one of the Army Mohawks crashed near the top of a 6000 foot mountain in the Central Highlands. Two Marine H-34 helicopters attempted to land a rescue team at the crash site, but as one hovered close to the tree tops it stalled and crashed, killing two of the occupants. The next morning another H-34 suffered the same fate, injuring two of the crew. Such fiascos illustrated the need for a properly trained and equipped Search and Rescue organization, but such a thing was almost two years in the future.

On 15 April 1963 two Martin RB-57E Canberras were deployed to Tan Son Nhut Air Base on Project *Patricia Lynn*. They were equipped with infrared and new panoramic cameras and the photographs that they brought back enabled photograph interpreters to identify such things as Viet Cong base camps, small arms factories and storage and training areas that were not otherwise detected by the naked eye. The Canberras joined the Tan Son Nhut

RF-101 force and were later supplemented by two *Farm Gate* RB-26s, modified for night photography, although these were withdrawn early in 1964 due to structural fatigue.

Two days after the B-57s arrived President Diem instituted his Chieu Hoi *open arms* campaign, a psychological (PSYOPS) warfare program designed to persuade members of the Viet Cong to defect to the government. This was carried out through leaflet drops or by using aircraft and helicopters equipped with loud-speakers to broadcast appeals for the guerrillas to surrender and return to their families. These often emotional appeals, together with a guarantee of clemency and financial inducements, persuaded many Viet Cong to defect to the government and some even worked as Kit Carson scouts for ARVN and later, American combat units. The Chieu Hoi campaign continued right through the war until, to the eternal shame of the CIA, the records of all the defectors were abandoned for the North Vietnamese to find as Saigon fell in 1975.

During the spring of 1963 there was a notable cooling of American-South

Vietnamese relations against the background of growing Buddhist opposition to President Diem. The problem came to a head in May when the Buddhists organized street demonstrations to protest against Diem's policies, in the ancient capital of Hue. The demonstrations were broken up by civil guards who opened fire on the Buddhists. During the next two months the unrest spread to Saigon where a Buddhist priest publicly burned himself to death in accordance with an ancient tradition. Despite attempts by the American Ambassador to persuade President Diem to modify his repressive rule, Diem's sister-in-law Madame Nhu continued to provoke the Buddhists with inflammatory statements. The Buddhists replied with more suicides.

The alternating *Water Glass* deployments of all-weather interceptors to Tan Son Nhut were terminated in May, due to the low probability of an enemy air attack and base overcrowding. A series of no-notice test deployments of Pacific

Air Force (PACAF) F-102s took place later in the year, under the new nickname *Candy Machine*.

The five original US Army CH-21 Transportation Companies began to re-equip with the UH-1B in the summer of 1963. The first unit to receive the new Hueys was the 81st Transportation Company at Pleiku, which was renamed the 119th Aviation Company (Air Mobile Light) on 14 June. By the end of the year most of the companies had re-equipped as the CH-21s were phased out of the Army inventory.

With the arrival of the UH-1Bs the structure of the Transportation Companies was changed and they were redesignated Aviation Companies. Each Company was made up of three platoons; two troop-lift or 'slick' platoons, (so named because their UH-1Bs lacked the drag-producing armament kits) and a platoon of UH-1B gunships. A total of 25 UH-1Bs was assigned to each Company; eight for each platoon, plus a reserve in the service platoon.

When the UH-1B transport helicopter was first introduced in Vietnam, it usually carried 10 or sometimes even 11 combat-equipped Vietnamese soldiers. An investigation determined that the average helicopter was grossly overloaded with this many soldiers. Each soldier averaged 167 pounds and with 10 on board a Huey, with a full load, a US Army crew of four, armor plate, a tool box, a container of water, a case of emergency rations, weapons and armored vests for the crew, the Huey grossed 8700 pounds, or 2100 pounds over normal gross weight and 200 pounds over the maximum operational weight. Not only that, the center of gravity had shifted beyond safe limits. As a consequence, the standard procedure was to limit the UH-1B to eight combat troops, except in the gravest emergencies.

The UTTHCO was the first to try out most new weapons or ideas for arming the UH-1B gunships. Apart from the early XM-6 system there were three basic weapon kits for the armed helicopter platoons during the early and middle years of US involvement in Vietnam. The XM-16 system combined the XM-6 with Navy and Air Force XM-157 seven-shot rocket pods. These became standard equipment in all gunship platoons, but the tubes were not individually replaceable and so repairs took longer to complete. In late 1965 the Army-developed XM-158

launcher was introduced with separate, removable tubes and safer rear loading. The impressive XM-3 system consisted of 48 rockets mounted in four six-tube banks each side of the helicopter. They were fired by either pilot or co-pilot through a Mark VIII reticle sight and could be launched in pairs, ripples of six pairs, or in a massive burst of all 24 pairs, delivering 480 pounds of explosives. The XM-5 grenade launcher was mounted in a ball-turret under the nose of the Huey and could fire 40mm grenades similar to those used in the infantry M-79 grenade launcher. The original system could fire a total of 150 rounds; 75 in a box in the rear cabin and a further 75 in the chute feeding system to the gun.

The armament system brought the UH-1B up to its maximum gross weight, thereby eliminating it from a troop or cargo-carrying role. The UH-1B was not actually designed for an armed configuration and the weight of armament system reduced the maneuverability of the aircraft and induced sufficient drag to lower the maximum speed to around 80 knots. As a result, the gunships could not overtake the airmobile force if they left the formation to attack targets en-route. The early armed UH-1Bs did an outstanding job in proving the concept of the armed helicopter, but they also highlighted deficiencies to correct in later versions.

Apart from armament, the UTTHCO tried and tested a wide range of tactics and formations. The basic fire team consisting of two gunships working together in support of each other

and the troop transport was developed. Several fire teams could be used together to support large formations, with some flying escort and the others going ahead to make pre-landing strikes at the landing zone (LZ) or to observe the LZ prior to the main assault. Some basic operating procedures became standard. When a target was identified the escort leader determined whether it could be attacked under the rules of engagement and if so, it was engaged at the maximum range of the gunships' weapons. This usually consisted of a continuous burst of machine-gun fire throughout each firing run, reinforced when necessary by rocket fire. The flight pattern was planned so that by the time the lead gunship had completed its firing run the next one was in position to engage the target. This tactic placed continuous fire on the target until it was neutralized.

Planning for an airmobile assault had evolved rapidly from the haphazard co-ordination witnessed in early 1962. Usually the Aviation Battalion would receive a mission request from the Corps Tactical Operations Center and then assign it to one of the Aviation Companies. If time permitted, an aerial reconnaissance was conducted by the airmobile company commanding officer, a representative of the Aviation Battalion and a representative from the supported unit. Approach and depar-

BELOW: A UH-1B Hog fitted with the XM-3 system of 24 2.75-inch folding-fin aerial rockets mounted each side of the fuselage.

ture routes were selected, condition and size of the LZ were noted and flight formations, check points and altitudes to be flown were determined. The type of helicopter formation to be used enroute depended basically on the size and shape of the LZ and the company commander's requirements for disembarking his troops after landing. When an uninterrupted flow of troops into a small landing area was required, a modified trail formation could be used. The formation most frequently used was the V. This proved to be versatile, easy to control and permitted landing of the flight in a minimum of time. The slicks normally flew about 45 degrees to the side and rear of the lead ship and high enough to be out of the rotor wash.

During the critical approach phase it was desirable to maneuver all the helicopters onto the ground simultaneously, although this was difficult due to the stepped altitude of the formation, the rotor wash encountered during descent and the difficulty in finding a suitable touchdown spot for each helicopter. The terrain in the LZ sometimes slowed the disembarking of troops. In the Delta, water was sometimes chest deep and in jungle areas the grass could be 10 to 12 feet high. For a 12-ship formation, two minutes were considered average unloading time from the moment the first helicopter touched down until the last ship took off. In a 'hot' landing zone where the assault is opposed by the enemy, two minutes can seem like an eternity. For obvious reasons the helicopters would take off in a different direction from their approach and to lessen the possibility of fire being concentrated on a single ship, all helicopters attempted to depart at the same time.

In an attempt to reduce the planning time required for executing an air assault mission, some of the earlier helicopter units developed a task force called an *Eagle Flight*. A typical *Eagle Flight* would consist of one armed Huey as the command and control ship, with the US Army aviation commander and the ARVN troop commander aboard; seven unarmed slicks to transport the combat troops; five armed Huey gunships to give fire support and escort the slicks and one Huey usually designated as a medical evacuation ship. The *Eagle Flights* were usually on standby or sometimes airborne searching for their own targets. Not only were the flights immediately available for missions with a minimum of planning, but they also provided the basis for larger operations. Several *Eagle Flights* were sometimes used against targets that, when developed, proved too large for a single unit.

By November 1964, all helicopter companies in South Vietnam had organized their own *Eagle Flights* and each company maintained at least one flight in an alert status on a continuing basis. The Vietnamese troop commanders were very enthusiastic about these operations, as they provided a very close working relationship between the air and ground elements and above all, were able to capitalize on the element of surprise which was so often lost in detailed planning with ARVN troops.

Although President Diem's armed

BELOW: Vietnamese troops board Marine H-34 helicopters from HMM-163 at Tam Ky.

forces were now performing better as a result of improved organization and training by their US advisers, Diem was facing problems in Saigon. The Buddhist demonstrations had continued through the summer and Diem decided it was time to teach them a lesson. On 21 August 1963 he sent his Special Forces and combat police to storm Buddhist pagodas throughout the country. Around 1400 men, mostly monks, were dragged off to jail where they were beaten, half starved and tortured. The American Embassy was shocked and horrified and within a week the Kennedy Administration, on CIA advice, had let it be known that they would back the generals who had long been planning a coup against Diem. These were led by General Doung Van Minh, 'Big Minh' as he became known to the Americans, and included General Tran Van Don, acting chief of the Joint General Staff and General Nguyen Khanh, commander of II Corps, north of Saigon.

On 1 November 1963 the generals launched their coup, spearheaded by two marine and two airborne battalions and backed by 30 tanks. They soon captured the radio station and other key buildings in Saigon, but Diem's loyal troops at the Presidential Palace put up a stiff resistance. In the meantime Wing Commander Nguyen Cao Ky had arrested the commander of the air force at Tan Son Nhut Air Base and sent two T-28s to attack the troops defending the Palace. After they had fired only two rockets the garrison surrendered, but not before Diem and his brother Nhu had escaped through a secret tunnel. They were eventually discovered in a Catholic church in Cholon, the Chinese city-within-a-city on the edge of Saigon. The brothers agreed to surrender following a guarantee of safe conduct and an armored car was sent to collect them. Their arms were bound and they were thrown into the armored car and then shot by a police officer. General Minh settled into the Presidential Palace as head of the Military Revolutionary Council and Ky was named as the new commander of the air force.

The new military rulers began the wholesale dismissal of government officials loyal to Diem and this action, together with their lack of administrative experience, soon produced governmental paralysis. The Viet Cong took advantage of the government's disarray and launched numerous attacks throughout South Vietnam. The de-

ABOVE: H-21s from the 57th Transportation Company (Light Helicopter).

moralized ARVN troops were no match for the enemy and suffered a number of defeats as a result.

In Cambodia Prince Norodom Sihanouk cancelled all American aid on 20 November and received four MiG jet fighters and 27 anti-aircraft guns from the Soviet Union. US activities within that country were to cease by 15 January 1964.

On 22 November 1963 President John F Kennedy was shot and killed in Dallas, Texas. Vice-President Lyndon B Johnson was inaugurated as President shortly afterward.

The year came to an end with the VNAF hard-pressed to respond to all requests for assistance. The *Farm Gate* detachment had been succeeded during the summer by 1st Air Commando Squadron, who were now facing problems with their B-26s. Structural fatigue in the wings had led to the fatal crash of a B-26 in August and the squadron was now under instructions to avoid undue wing stress.

American strength in South Vietnam had reached 16,000 and 117 USAF and 325 Army helicopters and aircraft were now based in the country. Casualties

had begun to mount and 18 USAF aircraft and 58 Army helicopters and aircraft had been lost to combat and to other non-hostile causes by the end of 1963.

On 18 January 1964 the ARVN launched the largest helicopter operation ever undertaken in South Vietnam up to that time. One hundred and fifteen helicopters were used to airlift 1100 troops into War Zone D. The operation went smoothly but unfortunately not a single Viet Cong soldier could be found.

Unsuccessful operations such as these, combined with continuing political instability, led to another coup on 30 January. Major General Nguyen Khanh, a tough paratrooper and commander of I Corps, ousted General Minh and stated his intention to increase operations against the enemy. However, such was the state of Vietnamese politics and the desire of the generals to dabble in politics that by the end of 1964 there had been seven changes of government.

While the Vietnamese generals indulged in political maneuvers, President Johnson settled himself in the executive chair at the White House and turned his attention to the war. On 21 February, in one of his first public comments on the war, President John-

son warned Hanoi to end its support of insurgent forces in South Vietnam and Laos. At this time he still supported the previous policy that the South Vietnamese and Laotian people were primarily responsible for their own defense. To this end the first withdrawal of 1000 US servicemen went ahead as planned. Among them were members of the famed *Dirty Thirty* group of C-47 pilots and the US Army's 1st Aviation Company.

In keeping with Washington's policy of expanding VNAF air capabilities so that US units and equipment could be withdrawn, MACV and 2nd Air Division were instructed to undertake a major review of the military situation. In the meantime, the 1st ACS with their ageing ground attack aircraft were in trouble. In February two of their T-28s were shot down by ground fire and ten days later their B-26s were grounded due to structural fatigue. General Jacob E Smart, the Commander-in-Chief, Pacific Air Forces, recommended deployment to South Vietnam of a B-57 light jet bomber squadron, but Secretary of Defense McNamara disagreed. He did however agree to equip a new VNAF squadron with Douglas A-1H Skyraiders and to replace the T-28s and B-26s of the 1st ACS with 25 two-seater A-1E Skyraiders.

These decisions came too late for two Air Force T-28 pilots and their Vietnamese crewmen. On 24 March one T-28 crashed after its wing sheared off during a bomb run and on 9 April a second T-28 ploughed into a rice paddy after both its wings fell off during a dive. General Moore, the 2nd Air Division Commander, noted that 'the 2nd Air Division is practically flat out of business' and the morale of the 1st ACS pilots sagged, despite the loan of nine surplus T-28Bs from the VNAF.

On 5 March Secretary McNamara approved the deployment of Detachment 6, 1st Air Commando Wing, to Udorn Royal Thai Air Force Base. The detachment, known by the nickname *Waterpump* consisted of four T-28s and 41 men and its mission was to train Laotian and Thai pilots and maintenance personnel. Not coincidentally, this unit also provided a source of US controlled aircraft to augment the small Royal Laotian Air Force and came directly under the control of US Ambassador Leonard Unger in Vientiane.

On 16 March all semblance of peace in Laos vanished as the Pathet Lao, with North Vietnamese backing, attacked across the Plain of Jars. As the Neutralist and Royal Laotian Government forces began to fall back, Washington approved the resumption of RF-101 reconnaissance flights on 19 May under the nickname *Yankee Team*. They were joined by US Navy RF-8A

Crusader and RA-3B Skywarrior reconnaissance aircraft from the Seventh Fleet in the Gulf of Tonkin.

Photograph interpreters scrutinizing *Yankee Team* photographs discovered that the Plain of Jars was bristling with anti-aircraft weapons and 16 37mm and 57mm sites were noted on or around the plain. These guns, capable of firing 150 rounds per minute, were effective up to 4500 and 15,000 feet respectively. Since most reconnaissance missions were flown below 1500 feet these powerful weapons were yet another threat to the unarmed reconnaissance pilots, who already had to contend with 12.7mm and 14.5mm heavy machine guns, with an effective range of 1800 and 3000 feet. The threat was realized on 6 June when *Corktip 920*, a Navy RF-8A piloted by Lieutenant Charles Klusmann, was shot down south of the village of Ban Ban, deep inside communist-controlled territory and only 20 miles from the North Vietnamese border. An Air America C-123 and U-10 Helio-Courier aircraft were in the area and located the pilot within an hour. Two hours later two Air America helicopters arrived at the crash scene, but as they approached the entire area erupted in gunfire. The enemy had employed a tactic he would use often during the next ten years; the flak trap. The pilot would be allowed to call for help while the enemy positioned anti-aircraft weapons around the area and waited for the rescuers to arrive. In this case both helicopters were hit and two men critically wounded. They had to abandon the attempt and head for the nearest Lima site (landing strip and base area). The following day *Old Nick 110*, an F-8D, was shot down in the same area while escorting an RF-8A on a reconnaissance mission. The pilot survived the ejection from his aircraft and spent a lonely night in the jungle evading the enemy. In the morning he heard the drone of aircraft above the foggy mist and fired a flare. An Air America H-34 helicopter descended below the clouds and snatched him to safety.

At this early stage of the war there

was no official co-ordinated Search and Rescue (SAR) organization to assist pilots who were shot down over South Vietnam or Laos. Of the two countries, Laos was worse to get shot down in and at the time of writing almost 600 American personnel are still listed as missing there. Fortunately Lieutenant Charles Klusmann, the pilot of *Corktip 920*, is not among them. After three months in captivity he managed to escape and reach safety on foot. The day after *Old Nick 110* was shot down, a retaliatory strike by eight USAF F-100 Super Sabres was authorized against the anti-aircraft sites at Xieng Khouang. From then on all RF-101 missions were given escorts of F-100s when their targets were on the Plain of Jars.

Pilots soon began to report large numbers of truck convoys along the Ho Chi Minh trail, although often their reconnaissance flights would be frustrated by bad flying weather. The annual monsoon season in Laos lasts from May to October and averages 50 inches of rainfall. Then the rain tapers

off and the cool season begins and continues through January. March brings warmer humid weather with temperatures that reach a high of 95 degrees in April, the hottest month. Dust, haze and smoke dominate the dry season when the Lao farmers practice their slash and burn agriculture. They set fire to their fields in preparation for the year's poppy planting and whirlwinds of smoke shoot hundreds of feet in the air, reducing visibility so much that in the words of one Air America pilot 'It was like flying around inside a milk bottle.'

Meanwhile, back in South Vietnam, the Viet Cong began to expand their military operations and at the same time, started to infiltrate regular North Vietnamese Army (NVA) units into the country. On 12 April they launched an attack on the district capital of Kien Long on the Ca Mau peninsula. Despite valiant air-to-ground support provided by VNAF A-1H Skyraiders, the Viet Cong overran the city, killing 300 ARVN troops and leaving over 200

BELOW: A pair of Royal Thai Air Force F-86 Sabres pictured during an exercise with USAF F-102 interceptors.

civilians dead or wounded. This defeat was followed by widespread terrorist attacks throughout the country, including a daring raid on 2 May when a Viet Cong underwater demolition team sank the USS *Card*, which had been unloading helicopters at the Saigon waterfront.

US Secretary of Defense McNamara visited Saigon in May and reiterated the administration's policy that all US airmen should be out of combat within a matter of months. He also decided that US Air Force pilots could no longer fly combat missions, even with a Vietnamese observer aboard, despite authorizing the Air Force to equip a second Air Commando Squadron with A-1Es. To balance this loss of USAF strike support he directed that four VNAF squadrons should be equipped with A-1Hs as soon as possible and that two more squadrons should be formed to replace the USAF units scheduled for withdrawal. Meanwhile, the situation at the 1st ACS began to improve as it received the first six A-1Es at the end of May, to replace its T-28s and B-26s.

The Skyraiders were well suited to the counter-insurgency role, with a 7000-pound bomb load, four 20mm cannon, heavy armor plating and an excellent loiter capability.

June 1964 saw a number of changes among the top-level commanders in Vietnam. General William Westmoreland replaced General Harkins as commander of the Military Assistance Command, Vietnam (MACV) and remained in the position until 1968, when he became Army Chief of Staff. Admiral Ulysses S Grant Sharp replaced Admiral Harry D Felt as Commander-in-Chief, Pacific (CINCPAC) and on the political front General Maxwell Taylor left his job as Chairman, Joint Chiefs of Staff, to replace Henry Cabot Lodge as US Ambassador to Vietnam.

June also saw the first efforts of establishing a Search and Rescue organization. Two Kaman HH-43B Huskie helicopters from the 33rd Air Rescue Squadron at Okinawa, arrived at Nakhon Phanom RTAFB on the Thai-Laos border. At the same time two

Grumman HU-16B Albatross amphibians were detached to Korat RTAFB to act as airborne rescue control ships and three HU-16Bs were sent to Da Nang in South Vietnam for rescue duties in the Gulf of Tonkin. While the arrival of the first SAR helicopters raised the morale of the *Yankee Team* reconnaissance pilots, the effect was not entirely warranted. The HH-43B was a short-range crash-rescue helicopter and the only one in the USAF inventory. It had a relatively small radius of action that varied between 125 and 140 miles and was thus unable to provide SAR cover for the Plain of Jars. An aircraft damaged by anti-aircraft fire over the Plain of Jars had to be flown at least 50 miles south to be within range of any rescue helicopters based at Nakhon Phanom. As the communist offensive in Northern Laos continued, it became obvious that the SAR assets were woe-

BELOW: A formation of USAF Super Sabres armed with napalm bombs pictured while on a mission over the Mekong Delta.

ABOVE: *Lil Miss Sweetness*, an RF-101C Voodoo ready for a reconnaissance mission from Tan Son Nhut.

fully inadequate to cover US air operations and Air America was asked to provide search and rescue support when needed. Air America's H-34 fleet had dwindled in numbers from 16 to four and in July they asked the Department of Defense for four more. These were transferred to them from the Fleet Marine Forces, Pacific, despite the protestations of CINCPAC. The Marines' objections were understandable. Medium Helicopter Squadron HMM-362 was the only Marine Corps squadron in Vietnam and was the resident Operation *Shufly* squadron at Da Nang. It had recently been given the job of training Vietnamese pilots and crews in the UH-34 and the Department of Defense directive came at the same time as HMM-362 was ordered to turn its 24

H-34's over to the VNAF, pending delivery of replacements from Sikorsky.

The Viet Cong turned July 1964 into the bloodiest month to date. On the 6th they attacked the Nam Dong Special Forces camp in I Corps, killing 55 ARVN troops, two US Rangers and an Australian adviser. Although a C-47 flare-ship illuminated the area, no VNAF strike aircraft were available to respond to calls for help. A fortnight later the Viet Cong ambushed 400 ARVN troops in Chuong Thien province in the Delta. It took an hour for a VNAF Forward Air Controller to arrive over the battle site and another half an hour before strike aircraft arrived from Bien Hoa. Only 82 ARVN soldiers walked away from the ambush.

In order to lessen the chances of another disaster by improving the air force response time to calls for help, MACV proposed to collate the Army Air Operations Section with the joint

USAF-VNAF Air Operations Center at Tan Son Nhut. Henceforth senior US Army advisers would hold a daily preplanning conference with their Air Force counterparts to ensure maximum use of the strike aircraft. An emergency VNAF air request net was also established to allow ARVN commanders to direct calls for help straight to an air support center, by-passing intermediate ARVN headquarters.

As the month of July 1964 came to an end, it was obvious that despite the assistance of over 16,000 American military advisers the South Vietnamese Army was unable to halt – let alone defeat – the Viet Cong insurgency. Regular North Vietnamese Army units were now being infiltrated into the South and it was time for the United States to raise the stakes. The opportunity to do so presented itself not in the jungles of South Vietnam, but on the high seas, in the Gulf of Tonkin.

3. Johnson's War

On 31 July 1964 the United States Navy began to conduct *DeSoto* intelligence gathering patrols along the coast of North Vietnam in the Gulf of Tonkin. This was in order to update their overall intelligence picture in case they had to operate against North Vietnam. The destroyer *Maddox* picked up the necessary equipment and personnel and headed north. At the same time, CIA-trained South Vietnamese commando squads operating from patrol craft, attacked North Vietnamese installations on Hon Me and Hon Ngu islands, 60 miles from the coast at the 19th parallel. Although the *Maddox* was 100 miles to the southeast at this time the raid stirred up a hornet's nest of electronic radio and radar activity sufficient to bring a smile to the face of even the hardest intelligence gathering equipment operator. Thirty-six hours later, on the morning of 2 August the *Maddox* arrived in the area having just received intelligence information that indicated possible action from North Vietnam. At 15.00 hours, while the *Maddox* was still supposedly in international waters, three North Vietnamese patrol boats came out to attack. As they engaged with torpedoes and machine-gun fire the *Maddox* requested assistance from the aircraft carrier USS *Ticonderoga*. Four F-8E Crusaders from Navy Fighter Squadron VF-53 were launched from the *Ticonderoga* and together with gunfire from the destroyer managed to sink or badly damage all three patrol boats.

High level discussions in Washington led to a decision to send the *Maddox* back into the area two days later on 4 August, together with the destroyer *C Turner Joy*. They were instructed to assert their right to sail in international waters up to eight miles from the North Vietnamese coast. By 20.00 hours on the night of the 4th, the destroyers were being buffeted by thunderstorms as they sailed through the darkness. The sonar on *Maddox* was functioning erratically and atmospheric conditions were distorting the signals reaching the radar on both ships. The *Maddox* intercepted a North Vietnamese message which was interpreted as implying that an attack was imminent. Eight Crusaders from the *Ticonderoga* were called up, but all failed to spot any attackers. Following a number of suspected contacts on the surface search radar, both ships opened fire on what they thought were torpedo boats only 6000 yards from the *Maddox*. Torpedo noises were heard on the *Maddox's* sonar and the crew of the *C Turner Joy* reported seeing a torpedo wake passing about 300 feet to port. Captain J J Herrick, the task force commander reported to his superiors that they were under attack and the message was passed on up the line to the President himself. By midnight radar contact with the enemy had ceased. Neither destroyer was damaged, although the *C Turner Joy* claimed three enemy boats sunk. As the destroyers left the area their commanders began to have doubts and suggested a thorough daylight reconnaissance by aircraft before any further action. The President and his advisers were convinced, however, that an attack had taken place and authorized retaliation against the North.

PAGES 50-51: A Super Sabre drops napalm on Viet Cong positions.
BELOW: A USAF C-130 Hercules lands at a busy Army airstrip.

The aircraft carrier USS *Constellation* had been ordered to leave Hong Kong on 2 August and proceed to the area at full speed. On both the *Ticonderoga* and *Constellation* crewmen hurried to arm and prepare their F-8 Crusaders, A-4 Skyhawks and A-1 Skyraiders for a 10.30 hours launch on 5 August. As President Johnson sat down before the television cameras to announce the raid to the nation, a message was flashed across the Pacific 'Launch *Pierce Arrow*.' Sixty-four naval aircraft struck four North Vietnamese patrol boat bases, destroying or damaging 25 boats; half of the North Vietnamese fleet. The fuel-oil storage tanks at Vinh, just north of the DMZ were struck, destroying 10 percent of the North's oil supply in one go. The raid was not without cost, however, as two Navy aircraft were lost. Before President Johnson had finished his speech, Lieutenant (j.g.) Everett Alvarez, a 26 year old Skyhawk pilot

LEFT: A US Navy A-1H Skyraider returns to the USS *Kitty Hawk* after a mission. The 'Spad' could carry 8000 pounds of ordnance.
BELOW: A C-130E starts its engines in the revetments at Saigon.

from the *Constellation*, was down in the water off Hon Gai with a fractured back. He became the first of 600 airmen to be captured during the war and was to spend eight years as a prisoner.

Two days after the reprisal raid, on 7 August, Congress passed the Southeast Asia Resolution, commonly called the Tonkin Gulf Resolution. This crucial and controversial document declared that,

> The United States regards as vital to its national interest and to world peace the maintenance of international peace and security in Southeast Asia. Consonant with the Constitution of the United States and the Charter of the United Nations and in accordance with its obligations under the Southeast Asia Collective Defense Treaty, the United States is, therefore, prepared, as the President determines, to take all necessary steps, including the use of armed force, to assist any member or protocol state of the Southeast Asia Collective Defense Treaty requesting assistance in defense of its freedom.
>
> This resolution shall expire when the President shall determine that the peace and security of the area is reasonably assured by international conditions created by action of the United Nations or otherwise, except that it may be terminated earlier by concurrent resolution of the Congress.

Thus did Congress give President Johnson and his advisers the power to direct an undeclared war against North Vietnam.

The United States had publicly announced its commitment to South Vietnam. The question now was 'What happens next?' The usual procedure once a government has decided to go to war, is to call in the military and tell them to get on with the job. The Joint Chiefs of Staff had drawn up contingency plans for American air operations against North Vietnam and they recommended a 'fast/full squeeze' hardhitting, sixteen-day air campaign against 94 targets in North Vietnam, to establish US air superiority and destroy Hanoi's ability to continue to support operations against South Vietnam. The military's view was to hit hard and right away. The Johnson Administration favored a campaign of gradually in-

LEFT: White Phosphorous bombs dropped by VNAF Skyraiders explode on VC positions.

creasing military pressures that would hopefully act as both 'carrot and stick' to induce North Vietnam to settle the war on US terms. No doubt Johnson was reluctant to commit himself to an all-out campaign with the elections only two months away, and he was also concerned that the destruction of Hanoi's war-making capability might bring China and Russia into the conflict. The JCS were aware of the possibility and assumed that communist Chinese ground troops might be used to aid the North Vietnamese, as had occurred in Korea and that Russia would provide increased military support including technicians and modern weaponry. They were confident, however, that the United States and its allies could deal adequately with such eventualities. The view of the President and his advisers prevailed and it was they, not the military who sat down to direct the air war, on a case by case and day by day basis.

The North Vietnamese were not impressed by the decisions of Congress, nor the reprisal raid on 5 August. Two days later they moved 30 MiG-15s and 17s into Phuc Yen airfield from China and ordered the 325th Division of the North Vietnamese Army south down the Ho Chi Minh trail.

The first USAF aircraft to deploy to South Vietnam following the Tonkin Gulf incident, were Martin B-57 Canberra bombers from the 8th and 13th Bomb Squadrons. They had been put on standby at Clark AB in the Philippines and during the evening of 4 August they were ordered to deploy 20 B-57Bs to Bien Hoa Air Base as soon as possible. They took the order literally and within hours the five flights of four aircraft had taken off and were en route to Vietnam. They arrived over Bien Hoa, an unfamiliar airfield, in darkness, and with a 700 foot ceiling of monsoon weather. Uncertainties after landing caused one aircraft to delay on the runway, whereupon it was struck by a second aircraft with brake failure and damaged beyond repair. Another B-57 blew both tyres on landing and the blocked runway caused the remaining B-57s to divert to Tan Son Nhut a few miles away. One B-57 did not arrive; it crashed a few miles short of the runway while on a straight-in TACAN approach. The crash site was in Viet Cong controlled territory and the reason for the crash was never satisfactorily determined.

The B-57B light bomber was a welcome addition to the USAF inventory in South Vietnam. It was armed with eight machine guns or four 20mm cannon and could carry an impressive bomb load on its underwing pylons and in its internal bomb bay. It could also carry eight 5-inch rockets or 28 2.75-inch rockets. This could be doubled if the wing bomb pylons were used. Unfortunately it was not used in combat for some time following its deployment. The United States was still abiding by the Geneva Agreement of 1954, which stipulated that no new military weaponry would be introduced in Vietnam by either side. It would be six months before the restriction was lifted and the B-57s were flown into combat.

Apart from the B-57s, other squadrons were on the move following the

BELOW: Aircraft of the Navy SP-2 Neptune *Market Time* detachment at Tan Son Nhut. RIGHT: A Navy Neptune checks out a junk for Viet Cong supplies.

Tonkin Gulf incident. Strike Force *One Buck* involved the deployment of 17 F-100 Super Sabres from the 614th Tactical Fighter Squadron (TFS) to Clark AB on 4 August and 18 more the next day from the 522nd TFS. Two months later the 614th TFS, a part of the 401st Tactical Fighter Wing (TFW), flew their F-100s on to Da Nang. Six more RF-101C Voodoos were sent to Tan Son Nhut Air Base to increase the *Able Mabel* detachment to 12, and other fighters moved into Thailand. These other fighters were Republic F-105 Thunderchiefs from the 18th TFW based on Okinawa. Within a week of the Tonkin Gulf incident eight F-105Ds were standing alert at Korat RTAFB on temporary duty (TDY). Their first combat mission took place before the end of August, when four F-105Ds from the 36th TFS were scrambled on a rescue combat air patrol (RESCAP). An aircraft had been reported downed over the Plain of Jars in Laos, but when the F-105s arrived they found an Air America C-7 Caribou orbiting the area who knew nothing about any bail-out, but said he was receiving anti-aircraft fire and asked the F-105s to knock out the gun site. They were unsure of the enemy position and decided to make strafing runs in the general area to tempt the enemy to show his hand and on the second pass he did just that. Lieutenant Dave Graben pressed the firing button as his big fighter hurtled toward the ground, spewing bursts of 20mm cannon fire from its Vulcan cannon at a rate of 6000 rounds per minute. Suddenly, in the pilot's words, 'red golf balls' streaked upward from the communists' 37mm anti-aircraft guns and the Thunderchief shuddered as the shells hit home. Graben pulled out of the steep dive and jettisoned all of his external stores and lit the afterburner to initiate a steep climb. The aircraft was vibrating badly and a red fire warning light came on as the pilot levelled out at 16,000 feet. Luck was with him as the warning light went out and the Thunderchief stayed in one piece to make a perfect landing back at Korat. The tail of the aircraft had been hit by two shells and there were also several shrapnel holes in the rear of the aircraft, but it had brought

ABOVE LEFT: Captain Larry Mason of the 8th Bomb Squadron inspects battle damage to his B-57 after landing at Da Nang.
LEFT: A fully-armed B-57B.

its pilot safely home. The *Thud* would continue to bring pilots home, with more severe damage than that suffered by Dave Graben and the type was soon in the forefront of the air war against North Vietnam.

One other deployment went almost unnoticed during the month of August. The first HH-43F rescue helicopters arrived at Bien Hoa and Da Nang to relieve the HH-43Bs. The newer model was a significant improvement with a more powerful engine, titanium armor plating and a 350-gallon self-sealing

ABOVE: A USAF F-100 performing road convoy escort duty.

RIGHT: The Viet Cong often fired on the 'Dustoff' UH-1 Medevac helicopters.

fuel tank which extended range from 75 to 120 nautical miles. It was also equipped with a newly developed jungle penetrator; a device which incorporated spring-loaded arms that parted jungle foliage as it was lowered to the survivor, who, after strapping himself to the penetrator released a set of spring-loaded arms at the other end to protect himself as he was hauled up through the branches of trees. This device was used throughout the war and was responsible for saving numerous survivors from the Southeast Asian rain forests. The HH-43Fs were still inadequate for the combat rescue mission, but six more months would pass before the first Sikorsky CH-3C helicopters, on loan from the Tactical Air Command, would arrive in Thailand.

Within a month of the *One Buck* deployment the US Army aviation inventory had grown to a total of 406 aircraft. The CH-21 Shawnees had all been replaced and 250 UH-1s were now in-country. The only other Army helicopter in use was the CH-37 Mojave cargo helicopter of which nine were employed. The other 147 aircraft consisted of 53 0-1 Bird Dogs, 20 U-6A Beavers, nine U-8 Seminoles, six OV-1

Mohawks, 32 C-7 Caribou and 27 U-1 Otters. Within a year though, the Army aviation inventory would expand beyond expectations as the Airmobile Division concept was put into practice.

At half past midnight on 1 November the Viet Cong infiltrated to within 250 yards of the perimeter wire at Bien Hoa Air Base. They silently emplaced six 81mm mortars, fired between 60 and 80 rounds into the base and departed, undetected and unmolested. Twenty B-57s were parked wingtip to wingtip on the ramp and five were totally destroyed, along with an HH-43F and four VNAF Skyraiders. All of the other 15 B-57s were damaged. Four Americans were killed and 72 others wounded. The JCS and the US Ambassador in South Vietnam strongly recommended retaliatory action against North Vietnam, but the White House declined; it was the eve of the 1964 Presidential elections. The retaliatory action pro-

RIGHT: A UH-1 of the 199th Infantry Brigade and an M-113 APC supporting American troops on a search and destroy operation.
BELOW: Sky troopers disembark from a 1st Cavalry Division (Airmobile) slick.

posed by the JCS involved a 24 to 36 hour period of air strikes in Laos and low-level air reconnaissance south of the 19th parallel in North Vietnam, to provide cover while US security forces were introduced to protect US bases and installations in South Vietnam. This would be followed by three days of B-52 strikes against Phuc Yen and other airfields and major fuel facilities in the Hanoi/Haiphong area. Subsequent strikes would be on infiltration routes and transportation-related targets in the North, together with raids against other military and industrial targets.

At this time the air defenses in the North were minimal. Apart from the few recently arrived MiGs the North

Vietnamese aircraft inventory comprised only 30 trainer and 50 transport aircraft and four light helicopters. Only Gia Lam Airfield at Hanoi and Cat Bi Airfield at Haiphong were capable of sustained jet operations, although Phuc Yen was nearly completed. Kien An at Haiphong and Dong Hoi, just north of the DMZ also had hard-surfaced runways capable of supporting jet aircraft. There were only around 700 conventional anti-aircraft weapons of all types and there were no surface-to-air missiles. The North Vietnamese radar

RIGHT: Two North Vietnamese MiG-17 jet fighters at Phuc Yen airfield near Hanoi.

tracking capability was limited and consisted of only 20 early warning sets with very little capability for definitive tracking. The US airstrikes would have been virtually unopposed and, launched with the element of surprise, they would have achieved the maximum success with a minimum number of losses. In the opinion of Admiral Sharp, CINCPAC at the time, such attacks would have had a major effect on North Vietnam and might well have persuaded North Vietnam to cease its aggression in the South. It was not to be. Eight more years would pass before the United States launched anything resembling an all-out attack on North Vietnam, and during that time period the North Vietnamese would build the largest, most powerful air defense system in the world.

The end of the year was marked by very heavy fighting on the ground. VNAF and USAF Skyraiders performed well and the air support units claimed 2500 Viet Cong killed in November and December, in addition to 1700 killed by government troops. The enemy losses were soon made good though, by replacements from the 30,000 to 40,000 infiltrators who had flowed into the south through Laos over the preceding three years.

In December President Johnson approved a series of limited armed reconnaissance missions against enemy lines of communication in eastern Laos, to signal his determination to counter Hanoi's increasing military activities and to bolster the morale of the governments of South Vietnam and Laos. The first mission of Operation *Barrel Roll* took place on 17 December when Navy aircraft from the carrier USS *Ranger* conducted an armed reconnaissance patrol over likely infiltration routes. The A-1H Skyraiders were escorted by F-4B Phantoms and followed by RF-8A photo-reconnaissance aircraft and were authorized to strike communist supply vehicles or other targets of opportunity. The purpose of these early *Barrel Roll* missions was mainly political and from the beginning Secretary McNamara allowed only two flights of four aircraft per week.

On Christmas Eve the Viet Cong blew up the Brink Hotel bachelor officers' quarters in Saigon, killing two Ameri-

RIGHT: A door gunner wearing the shoulder patch of the 1st Aviation Brigade, holds his M-60 at the ready.

cans and injuring 71 others. The Commander USMACV, CINCPAC and the JCS all requested an airstrike against North Vietnam as a reprisal, but the Johnson administration refused. Three days later the Viet Cong 9th Division, recently formed and supplied with Soviet and Chinese weapons brought in by sea, attacked Binh Gia village, southeast of Saigon. The battle led to the virtual destruction of the government's 33rd Ranger and 4th Marine Battalions and to heavy losses among the relief column. The Viet Cong later boasted that the battle marked the end of the insurgency phase of its campaign and the beginning of conventional field operations.

As 1965 began the US military commanders convinced President Johnson that stronger action was needed against North Vietnam. An excuse for such stronger action was provided on 7

February when the Viet Cong attacked the American compound and airstrip at Camp Holloway near Pleiku in the early hours of the morning. Eight Americans were killed and 100 others wounded; five helicopters were destroyed. An hour later the Viet Cong attacked and set fire to aviation fuel storage tanks at Tuy Hoa airfield, but in this instance there were no casualties. President Johnson ordered all US military dependents to leave Vietnam as he 'cleared the decks' and ordered a retaliatory raid against North Vietnam.

At midday on 7 February 1965, little more than 12 hours after the Pleiku incident, 49 A-1 Skyraiders and F-8 Crusaders took off from the decks of the USS *Coral Sea* and *Ranger*; Operation *Flaming Dart I* had begun. Their target was the North Vietnamese Army barracks and guerrilla training establishment at Dong Hoi. Thirty-four other

ABOVE: A UH-1B gunship from the Mustang platoon of D Troop, 4th Cavalry, fitted with the XM-16 armament system.

aircraft were launched from the USS *Ranger* and headed for the barracks at Vit Thu Lu, 15 miles inland. The force from the *Ranger* could not hit their target because of the monsoon weather, but much of the Dong Hoi barracks was destroyed. In an attempt to boost South Vietnamese morale the VNAF was invited to participate in the operation, but when their force of 24 A-1 Skyraiders arrived over Dong Hoi they found the Navy attack in full swing and decided to find another target to punish. The VNAF contingent was commanded by Air Marshal Ky, the chief of the VNAF himself, and he led his force away to attack a target in the Vinhlinh area. Their target was the headquarters of an

RIGHT: The engine of this F-8 of VF-154 flamed out near the USS *Coral Sea*.
MIDDLE: The pilot ejects to be picked up after only 80 seconds in the water.
BOTTOM: South Vietnamese Prime Minister Ky on board the *Independence*.

anti-aircraft regiment and the return fire was ferocious. Every one of the aircraft received hits, including Air Marshal Ky who was grazed by a bullet, and two pilots were forced to bail out over the sea. The VNAF attack caused some friction between Saigon and Washington as the target had not been authorized, but Ky lost no sleep over this; he knew that there was a war going on. The US Air Force joined in the following day, 8 February, when 30 *Farm Gate* A-1s accompanied by F-100s flying flak suppression missions, struck the barracks at Chap Le. The President, emphasizing that the air strikes were reprisals for the earlier attacks, reiterated that the United States sought no wider war.

The Viet Cong replied two days later when they blew up a hotel being used as enlisted men's quarters in Qui Nhon, killing 23 American soldiers and wounding many more. The next day Operation *Flaming Dart II* began when 99 strike aircraft launched from the three aircraft carriers in the South China Sea. Their targets were the barracks at Vit Thu Lu and Chanh Hoa, 35 miles north of the DMZ. The weather was bad as the northeast monsoon which lasts from November to April, was at its height. The Navy aircraft roared in to the attack at Chanh Hoa despite 500 foot ceilings and less than one mile visibility. Three aircraft were shot down with one pilot captured and the other two rescued. The North Vietnamese were unimpressed by the raids and continued their attacks.

The US Navy was to employ the McDonnell Douglas A-4 Skyhawk and the Ling Temco Vought F-8 Crusader throughout the whole of the Vietnam War. The A-4 was a small single-seat light attack aircraft, powered by a 8500-pound thrust Pratt and Whitney J52 turbojet (A-4E), giving it a range of 700 miles and a maximum speed at sea level of 675mph. The *Scooter* as it was often called, was armed with two 20mm cannon mounted in the wing roots and could carry up to 8200 pounds of ordnance on its underwing and center-line pylons. Both the Marine Corps and the Navy used the A-4C and E, with the

latter sustaining most of the losses throughout the war. The A-4 flew more bombing missions than any other naval aircraft and by the end of the war a total of 374 from both services had been lost to all causes. Lieutenant Alvarez had been flying an A-4C on 5 August 1964 when he became the first Navy pilot to be captured by the North Vietnamese and the first Navy aircraft to be brought down by a surface-to-air missile (SAM) was an A-4E a year later on 13 August 1965.

During the early years of the Vietnam War the Crusader was the principal US Navy fighter aircraft and the type is credited with the destruction of 18 North Vietnamese fighters. A single-seat aircraft powered by a Pratt and Whitney J-57 engine the F-8C had a range of 320 miles and was armed with four 20mm cannon and four fuselage mounted AIM-9 Sidewinder air-to-air missiles. The improved F-8E had a greater range of 350 miles and was also

LEFT: Railroad cars destroyed south of Thanh Hoa by Skyhawks from the *Oriskany*.
BELOW: Fuel tanks burn in Haiphong after a visit by aircraft from the *Oriskany*.

ABOVE: AIM-9 Sidewinder air-to-air missiles being fitted on to an F-8 Crusader aboard the aircraft carrier *Hancock*.

equipped to fire the air-to-ground Bull-pup missile. It had a heavier, reinforced wing and underwing pylons which could carry extra fuel tanks, missiles, rockets, bombs or electronic counter-measures (ECM) pods. The Marine Corps also used the F-8E in the close air support role and lost 23 to all causes during the war. The Navy made greater use of the Crusader and lost 114 together with 29 reconnaissance RF-8 models, to all causes; that is to hostile action and for other reasons.

The composition of a carrier air wing depended on its area of operations and the size of the carrier. The USS *Bon Homme Richard* embarked Air Wing 19 for its west Pacific cruise and combat operations off Vietnam between April 1965 and January 1966. This typical Air Wing consisted of two squadrons of F-8Es, two squadrons of A-4s and a third attack squadron flying A-1 Skyraiders. A photo-reconnaissance detachment flew the RF-8 Crusader, while airborne early-warning was provided by the Grumman E-1B Tracer and ECM

escort by the EA-1F conversion of the Skyraider. A number of Kaman UH-2A Seasprite helicopters were also embarked for rescue and utility duties.

Another Navy operation which began in February 1965 was *Market Time*, a surface and air patrol effort to reduce the seaborne infiltration into South Vietnam of communist arms and supplies. The enemy supply effort was directed by North Vietnamese Naval Transportation Group 125, which used steel-hulled, 100-ton trawlers and seagoing junks to bring the supplies direct to the Viet Cong waiting on the beaches, or to transfer their loads onto smaller junks, sampans and other craft. The coastal surveillance operation covered the 1200-mile South Vietnamese coast from the 17th parallel to the Cambodian border and extended 40 miles out to sea. Within this area surface search was conducted by ships of the US Navy, US Coast Guard and the South Vietnamese Navy. American aircraft operating from ships offshore and from bases in South Vietnam, Thailand and the Philippines carried out air search of the *Market Time* area. For a brief time in 1965 A-1 Skyraiders based on aircraft carriers at *Dixie Station* flew surveillance missions along

the coast. This mission was shared and then taken over by a patrol squadron based at Sangley Point in the Philippines equipped with the advanced P-3 Orion aircraft. Throughout this period five to seven SP-2H Neptune aircraft were stationed at Tan Son Nhut Air Base and made regular patrols up and down the South Vietnamese coast.

In addition, from May 1965 to April 1967 ageing Martin SP-5 Marlin seaplanes operated from the seaplane tenders *Currituck* and *Salisbury Sound* anchored at Condore and Cham islands or at Cam Ranh Bay. When the seaplanes were withdrawn early in 1967, a squadron of 12 Neptunes was stationed ashore at Cam Ranh Bay and a detachment of P-3s began coverage of the Gulf of Siam from U Tapao RTAFB in Thailand. The *Market Time* surveillance operation actually involved three different missions. Apart from seeking out communist supply vessels, the patrol aircraft were used to shadow Russian and Chinese ships and to keep watch for any enemy torpedo boats or aircraft which might pose a threat to the ships on *Yankee Station* in the Gulf of Tonkin. However, as the effectiveness of *Market Time* increased the communists developed less costly and

ABOVE: *Big Eye* EC-121s provided radar coverage over North Vietnam and Laos.
LEFT: A Navy Grumman E-2A Hawkeye from one of the aircraft carrier AEW detachments.

more efficient means of supplying their forces in the South. From December 1966 onward the port of Sihanoukville in supposedly neutral Cambodia was used as a secure transhipment point for enemy munitions destined for the Mekong Delta battleground. In addition the Ho Chi Minh Trail had become a well-established supply system that sustained the needs of the communist units operating in the I and II Corps areas. By the time decisive action was taken in 1970 and 1971 to try to close these alternate supply routes for good, it was too late to effect the outcome of the war.

As the plans were being made for the first *Market Time* missions, authority was at last given to use the B-57s at Bien Hoa on combat missions and without the need to have a VNAF crewman on board. Technically, it was a violation of the 1954 Geneva Agreement, but the United States and South Vietnam felt that, since the North Vietnamese had violated the agreement, then they could too. At 14.30 hours on 19 February the first of 18 B-57s from the 8th and 13th Bomb Squadrons took off from Bien Hoa. Twenty minutes later they were

ABOVE: An F-4C Phantom from the 366th TFW *Gunfighters* based at Da Nang.
RIGHT: A CH-47 Chinook prepares to lift a disabled Huey.

over the target, a suspected Viet Cong concentration near Binh Gia, about 30 miles east of Saigon, and the scene of the heavy fighting two months previously. As the crews completed their bomb-runs a number of secondary explosions were noted, indicating that fuel or ammunition caches had also been hit. All aircraft returned home safely as F-100s carried on the attack. Two days later the B-57s and F-100s were scrambled to assist a US Army Special Forces team and a CIDG (Civilian Irregular Defense Group) company which had been ambushed at the Mang Yang pass on Route 19, east of Pleiku. The close air support prevented the enemy from overrunning the Allied forces while US helicopters moved in and evacuated the 220 men who might otherwise have been lost.

Back in Washington officials no longer talked about withdrawing US advisers from South Vietnam, rather they recommended the deployment of additional US forces. Soon, two B-52 Stratofortress squadrons belonging to the Strategic Air Command were on their way to Andersen Air Force Base on Guam for possible use over South

Vietnam. Nine more USAF Tactical Fighter Squadrons were alerted for deployment, a fourth aircraft carrier was despatched to the South China Sea and on 13 February 1965 President Johnson approved the inauguration of an air warfare campaign against North Vietnam.

In Laos the joint Navy and Air Force *Barrel Roll* force was redirected toward key transport bottlenecks or 'choke' points on the Ho Chi Minh Trail. The first such attack was carried out on 28 February when Skyraiders and Skyhawks from the USS *Coral Sea* attacked the road through the Mu Gia Pass near the border of North Vietnam and Laos. Although the supply route was repeatedly cut at critical points, the North Vietnamese soon managed to repair the

roads, construct bypasses and maintain the logistical flow. It was obvious stronger action was needed.

The main attack on the North was not to be an all-out, short sharp campaign using strength and surprise, but rather a slow gradual program of attacks, increasing in intensity over the months with the aim of persuading Hanoi to negotiate an end to its insurgency in the South. It was not what the President's military advisers wanted but, at the time, at least it was a step in the right direction. The campaign was to be known as *Rolling Thunder* and would continue, with various pauses, for the next four years. The first four *Rolling Thunder* strikes were cancelled because the attention of the South Vietnamese armed forces was focused on the possi-

ABOVE: The USS *Coral Sea* returns home after 331 days in the western Pacific, flying over 160 strike missions.

bility of another coup. The VNAF was thus unavailable to join with US forces in the air strikes, a mandatory requirement at that time, although the requirement was soon dropped as the campaign got underway. The first *Rolling Thunder* strike took place on 2 March against the Xom Bong ammunition dump and the small naval base at Quang Khe, about 35 miles north of the DMZ. The attacking force consisted of 44 F-105s, 40 F-100s, 20 B-57s and seven RF-101Cs to take post-strike photographs of the bomb damage. They were accompanied by a nominal VNAF force of 19 aircraft. All the USAF aircraft were based in South Vietnam with the exception of the F-105s which were from the 12th and 67th TFS at Kadena Air Base, Okinawa and on temporary detachment to bases in Thailand. Three of the F-105s and two F-100s were shot down by enemy ground fire and Captain Hayden J Lockhart became the first USAF pilot to be captured by the North Vietnamese.

The JCS and CINCPAC were disturbed by the assignment of such insignificant targets and the long delays between strikes. Ambassador Taylor echoed their thoughts in a message to Washington on 8 March.

It appears to me evident that to date DRV (North Vietnam) believe air strikes at present levels on their country are meaningless and that we are more susceptible to international pressure for negotiations than they are. Their estimate may be based in part on activities of our friends to which we seem to be an active party. In my view current developments strongly suggest that we follow simultaneously two courses of action. First, attempt to apply brakes to the British and others in their headlong dash to the conference table until there is clear evidence that Hanoi (and Peking) are prepared to leave their neighbors alone; and, two, step up the tempo and intensity of our air strikes in the southern part of DRV in order to convince Hanoi authorities they face the prospect of progressively severe punishment. I fear that to date *Rolling Thunder* in their eyes has merely been a few isolated thunder claps . . .

As Ambassador Taylor was drafting his message to Washington a significant event was taking place on the ground. At 06.00 hours on 8 March 1965 the commander of the Seventh Fleet's Amphibious Task Force issued the traditional order to 'Land the landing the force' and 3500 men of the 9th Marine Expeditionary Brigade began to file into their landing craft. At 09.00 hours the first Marines waded ashore at Da Nang to be greeted by garland-carrying Vietnamese girls. The 3rd Battalion, 9th Marines became the first US combat unit to deploy to South Vietnam. They were there initially to protect the US base at Da Nang, but within a month they began to move out and engage Viet Cong and North Vietnamese forces in combat.

The second USAF *Rolling Thunder* strike did not take place until the 15th and two days later the Navy joined in. On 18 March aircraft from the USS *Hancock* and *Coral Sea* bombed supply

BELOW: The seaplane tender USS *Salisbury Sound* with a Martin SP-5B Marlin aboard.

buildings at Phu Van and Vinh Son. Target allocation remained slow and strictly controlled by Washington, who even decided the timing of the raids and how many aircraft would be used and with which armament; decisions which should have been made by the experienced Air Force and Navy commanders in the theater of operations. At this time the targets were all in the southernmost part of North Vietnam, such as barracks, radar sites, ammunition depots and military vehicles. Meanwhile the JCS emphasized the need to interdict the North Vietnamese lines of communication (LOCs) to reduce the flow of men and material into South Vietnam. The JCS recommended the destruction of the southern portion of the North Vietnamese rail system, of which 115 miles extended below the 20th parallel. The prime targets in the system were the rail yards at Vinh and five large bridges including the Dang Phuon Rail

ABOVE: The Douglas A-3 Skywarrior was used as a strike aircraft on a limited basis.
RIGHT: A USAF F-100 Super Sabre firing a pod of folding-fin rockets.

and Highway Bridge and the Thanh Hoa bridge. The latter two bridges were earmarked for destruction first, in order to trap the maximum amount of rolling stock south of the 20th parallel where it could then be destroyed.

In an attempt to define a strategy for crippling the war-making capability of North Vietnam, the JCS submitted a four-phase program to Secretary of Defense McNamara, incorporating the destruction of the southern part of the rail system. The idea was to isolate the North from external sources of resupply and then to destroy her internal military and industrial capacity. Phase One (three weeks) was aimed at interdicting all LOCs south of

the 20th parallel, starting with an attack on the Thanh Hoa Rail and Highway Bridge. Phase Two (six weeks) called for severing all rail and highway links with China, including the destruction of the Paul Doumer Rail and Highway Bridge. Phase Three (two weeks) involved air attacks against all port facilities, the mining of seaward approaches and the destruction of ammunition and supply dumps. Phase Four (two weeks) was the wind-up phase, devoted to restriking all the previous targets as necessary, as well as attacks on industrial targets that were outside populated areas.

The initial targets in the campaign were to be the key bridges in the North Vietnamese railroad system, which comprised five major lines, as follows: (i) the 140 mile northwest rail line connecting Hanoi with the south-central Chinese rail system; (ii) the 82 mile northeast rail line which provided an important rail link between the south-eastern Chinese supply concentrations and Hanoi; (iii) the 40 mile eastern rail link between Hanoi and North Vietnam's major port city, Haiphong; (iv) the 165 mile southern rail line, extending from Hanoi south through Thanh Hoa and Vinh to the DMZ and (v) a 45 mile stretch of track from a mining area north of Thai Nguyen to the northeast rail line 10 miles north of Hanoi, which served the Thai Nguyen iron and steel complex. The Achilles Heel of the rail system lay on the outskirts of Hanoi where four of the five major rail lines came together to cross the Red River on the Paul Doumer Railroad and Highway Bridge. Destruction of this bridge would sever Hanoi from China and the major North Vietnamese seaport at Haiphong. It would also interdict National Route 1, the most important highway leading north from Hanoi. With this route cut all truck traffic would have to be rerouted to National Routes 2 and 3, northwest of Hanoi and served by a ferry across the Red River. All Haiphong to Hanoi road traffic would also have to be ferried across the Red River. The JCS stressed that any delay in authorizing the destruction of the Paul Doumer Bridge would allow the enemy time to build an extensive bypass system of river ferries and to develop an effective air defense system to protect the bridge.

President Johnson and his advisers would not approve the 13-week bombing program recommended by the JCS and the Paul Doumer Bridge remained 'off limits' until August 1967. They did, however, approve a campaign against the southern rail network and first on the list of targets was the Thanh Hoa railroad and highway bridge, known to the Vietnamese as Ham Rong (the Dragon's Jaw). The first raid on the bridge took place on 3 April and involved 79 aircraft; 46 F-105s, 21 F-100s, 2 RF-101s and 10 KC-135 tankers. Sixteen of the 46 F-105s were loaded with a pair of Bullpup missiles and each of the remaining 30 carried eight 750-pound general purpose bombs. The aircraft that carried the missiles and half of the bombers were scheduled to strike the bridge; the remaining 15 would provide flak suppression. Seven of the F-100s were also assigned to flak suppression, two to

BELOW: A 363rd TRW RB-66 at Tan Son Nhut.
BOTTOM: US Ambassador Maxwell Taylor addresses troops of the 101st Airborne Division. General Westmoreland looks on.

ABOVE: An F-105D Thunderchief with six bombs and two underwing drop tanks.

weather reconnaissance, four to provide MiG CAP (Combat Air Patrol) and eight to be used for rescue top cover (RESCAP) if required. The RESCAP and flak suppression F-100s each carried two pods of 19 2.75-inch rockets, and the latter also had two 750-pound bombs for good measure. The MiG CAP F-100s were armed with Sidewinder missiles and the whole force of fighters was equipped with 20mm cannons. The F-100s flew up the coast from South Vietnam while the F-105s from Thailand refueled in the air over the Mekong River.

At 14.00 hours the flak suppression flights began the attack and their bombs and rockets were still exploding around the anti-aircraft emplacements as the

Bullpup-carrying Thunderchiefs appeared on the scene. The Bullpups were released at 12,000 feet and streaked earthward as the pilots guided them on to the bridge. The missiles had to be fired one at a time and as the pilots prepared to go around once again, they were surprised to see no visible damage to the bridge. The bomb-carrying F-105s released their loads in a dive at 4000 feet and headed for home. Post-strike photography confirmed that the bridge had taken numerous hits from the 32 missiles and 120 bombs, but only the roadway on the south side had incurred significant damage. The highway on the northern side and the railroad in the center would require only minor repairs. The lack of success was no reflection on the pilots because the bridge had been, architecturally, grossly overbuilt. It was a replacement for the original French-built bridge

which had been destroyed by the Viet Minh in 1945; they had simply loaded two locomotives with explosives and ran them together in the middle of the bridge. The new bridge was 540 feet long and 56 feet wide and comprised two steel thru-truss spans which rested in the center on a massive reinforced concrete pier, 16 feet in diameter, and on concrete abutments 30 to 40 feet thick, anchored into the hillsides. The center pier only supported the middle 12 feet of the bridge containing the railroad, the 22 feet highway lanes cantilevered on each side were expendable and easily repaired. Heavy weapons would have to be dropped along the middle 12 feet of the bridge to make it fall and although such accurate weapons were not available until May 1972, the Air Force prepared to strike the bridge again the following day.

On 4 April the bridge was attacked

again by 48 F-105s carrying eight 750-pound bombs each. Three hundred bombs hit the target and the bridge was severely damaged. The 750-pounders though, were just not powerful enough and within a month the rail line was in use again. Three F-105s were lost that day; two were in the last flight scheduled to strike the bridge and were shot down by four MiG-17s who came out of the clouds with their cannons blazing and then continued out of the area at maximum speed. These were the first USAF aircraft to fall to the enemy MiGs. The third F-105 was hit by anti-aircraft fire and as the aircraft shuddered and went out of control Captain 'Smitty' Harris baled out to face seven years in a prisoner of war camp. It was the curse of the 'Thud' that it was prone to loss of control when the hydraulic system took even the smallest of hits. Within seconds the hydraulic fluid would be gone, leaving none to power the flight controls and no way to steer the aircraft out of the area. A simple back-up system could have given many pilots the chance to head for a safer bail-out area, preferably 'feet wet' over the Gulf of Tonkin where the ships of Task Force 77 waited. Such a modification finally came through, but it was too late for many brave pilots.

Following a fact-finding mission to South Vietnam by General Harold Johnson, the Army Chief of Staff, the President relaxed some of the bombing restrictions. Targets were now selected in weekly packages with the timing of the attacks left to the local commander. Armed reconnaissance missions to hunt for targets of opportunity were allowed and flak-suppression and combat air patrol aircraft were now permitted to attack other targets on the way home from the target area.

The loss of the two F-105s to the MiG-17s on 4 April was of some concern to the Air Force. They had obviously been vectored to the F-105 flight by a ground controlled intercept (GCI) radar unit. The MiGs then carried out their attack and broke away for home before the surviving F-105s could engage them. To provide advance warning of such attacks in future, a detachment of Lockheed EC-121Ds from the 552nd Airborne Early Warning and Control Wing was sent to Tan Son Nhut Air Base. They were equipped with search radar and radio relay transmitters and became an airborne extension to the TACS radar net. The EC-121s of the *Big Eye* (later

College Eye) task force began to fly orbits over the Gulf of Tonkin and Laos, providing radar coverage over North Vietnam and Laos. They could determine the range and altitude of hostile aircraft and issue advance warnings to friendly aircraft. The MiG warning at that time was given via a color code; yellow signified that MiGs were airborne and red meant that they were about 10 minutes away from a possible engagement.

The effectiveness of MiG combat air patrols was also increased by the arrival in Thailand of the first McDonnell Douglas F-4C Phantoms. The 18 aircraft from the 45th TFS of the 15th TFW left MacDill AFB in Florida on 4 April and flew to Ubon RTAFB, followed three months later by the 47th TFS. The two-seater Phantom included a less-experienced pilot in the back seat, called a pilot systems operator (PSO) who also operated the radar. Known as the GIB or *guy in back*, the official term was later altered to navigator/weapon systems officer (WSO) when it was decided that the back seater should be a non-rated flyer. Although the F-4C carried air-to-air missiles and, later on, detachable gun pods, at this time it was not armed with guns; a distinct disadvantage when it came to engage in dogfights with the enemy MiGs.

Over the border in Laos, Operation *Steel Tiger* began on 1 April 1965 as a day and night air campaign against enemy troops and supply vehicles in the

southern panhandle of Laos. It was preceded, from December 1964, by Operation *Barrel Roll*, a daytime campaign, and was aimed at disrupting the communist supply lines down the Ho Chi Minh Trail to South Vietnam. Both Navy and Air Force aircraft were used during the daytime, but the night intruder missions were flown exclusively by B-57 bombers. The first of these launched the campaign on 1 April when two B-57s joined a *Blind Bat* C-130 flare ship in the area of Tchepone, where the supply routes filtered in from North Vietnam. By the end of the night the B-57s had destroyed a ferry boat with four trucks on it, one bridge and 20 buildings by secondary explosions

LEFT: An SP-5B Marlin from Patrol Squadron VP-40 searches for Viet Cong junks.
BELOW: F-105Ds from the 388th TFW refuel from a KC-135 tanker.

(caused by exploding ammunition or fuel). A detachment of Douglas EF-10B Skyknight aircraft from Marine Composite Reconnaissance Squadron VMCJ-1 arrived at Da Nang on 10 April. They began to accompany the night bombers on their missions, to jam radar controlled anti-aircraft weapons and detect hot missile sites that might be preparing to launch. In July the first of the ageing EF-10s was lost when it crashed into the sea and four others were lost during the war to enemy fire; three in South Vietnam and one over the North. The type continued to fly electronic-warfare missions over Laos and North Vietnam until 1969, when it was replaced by the Grumman EA-6A Intruder which had more sophisticated electronics.

The day after the first EF-10s flew into Da Nang the first Marine Corps F-4B Phantoms arrived. They were from Fighter Attack Squadron VMFA-531 from Atsugi in Japan and they carried out their first combat mission the next day. The F-4B was armed with air-to-air missiles and although it carried no gun, it could carry up to 16,000 pounds of ordnance including bombs, Bullpup air-to-surface missiles and packs of 2.75-inch folding-fin rockets. Soon the Marines' Phantoms began to perform their duties as close-support aircraft for the Marine combat troops, as the 'grunts' began to move into the countryside to engage the enemy.

On 15 April 1965 Navy carrier aircraft went into action in South Vietnam with a strike against Viet Cong positions near Black Virgin Mountain. The USMACV commander, General Westmoreland, was so impressed with the Navy's support that he asked for an aircraft carrier to be stationed off South Vietnam. Consequently, *Dixie Station* was established and Navy carrier air-

ABOVE: A North Vietnamese pilot poses for a photograph in front of his MiG fighter.
LEFT: North Vietnamese pilots undergoing training in the Soviet Union.

craft began to fly regular combat missions in-country on 20 May 1965. *Dixie* operations continued until 4 August 1966 when land-based aircraft were well enough established to handle most of the required air support in the South. *Dixie Station* was also used as a warming-up area for newly arrived carrier air wings. In the comparatively peaceful southern war zone the green air crews could get used to flying in combat, before going North into the real world of AAA, SAMs and MiGs. A geographical point in the Gulf of Tonkin was designated *Yankee Station* and served as a central location for carrier operations against the North.

By June 1965 five aircraft carriers were on line flying dozens of missions daily as a part of *Rolling Thunder*.

It was an RF-8A Crusader from the USS *Coral Sea* which brought back aerial photographs of the first surface-to-air missile (SAM) site on 5 April. The site was 15 miles southeast of Hanoi and its discovery led the commander of Task Force 77 on *Yankee Station* to fly to Saigon to discuss the new development with the commander of the Seventh Air Force. Both men recommended an immediate strike against the site but permission was refused. More sites were established over the coming months, but six months were to elapse before the first SAM site was destroyed. In the meantime both Navy and Air Force aircraft and crews had been lost to the new SA-2 Guideline missile and the air war over the North had become a whole new ball game.

The first six Douglas RB-66C Destroyer aircraft arrived in April to perform Early Warning, Intelligence gathering and ECM duties over North Vietnam. They were from the 41st Tactical Reconnaissance Squadron (TRS) and were joined in October by five more from the 6460th TRS. Another type new to the theater was the Lockheed F-104 Starfighter. The 476th TFS deployed its 24 F-104s from George AFB in California to Taiwan and Da Nang during April and began to fly missions over North Vietnam and Laos. By the end of 1967 fourteen Starfighters had been lost including two which suffered a mid-air collision over South Vietnam in September 1965. The USAF also activated four 0-1 Bird Dog squadrons in South Vietnam during April and reinforced the F-105 units in Thailand with the 563rd TFS and 421st TFS, both with 18 aircraft each. The 421st was a part of the 355th TFW and that wing's other four squadrons also deployed to Takhli RTAFB between October 1965 and January 1966. Eventually the F-105 units on temporary duty were replaced by the 355th TFW and the 388th TFW which moved into Korat RTAFB in April 1966. Each wing had around 55 F-105s and out of the total of 110, approximately 80 to 85 were available each day to fly combat missions.

By mid-1965, despite the poor weather caused by the southwest monsoon which sweeps over Laos between May and October, US Navy and Air Force pilots were flying over 1000 *Steel Tiger* sorties each month. South Vietnamese ground reconnaissance teams, led by US Green Berets, were sent into the border areas to try to pinpoint enemy traffic on the Ho Chi Minh trail and were soon directing strikes against truck parks and supply dumps normally concealed from the air by the jungle growth or bad weather. In order to provide a faster response against fleeting targets, the Air Force began to place F-105 *Whiplash* flights on standby alert at some of the bases in Thailand. Despite the best efforts of the USAF, by the end of the year the North Vietnamese were infiltrating over 4500 men and 300 tons of supplies monthly into South Vietnam.

On 4 May 1965 the 173rd Airborne Brigade began to arrive at Bien Hoa from Okinawa. One hundred and forty two sorties were required to move the Brigade which was tasked to provide security for Bien Hoa and Vung Tau Air Bases. The 173rd was the first US Army combat unit to arrive in Vietnam,

BELOW: A USAF Sikorsky HH-3E *Jolly Green Giant* plucks a downed pilot from the sea.

but during the month the number of US servicemen in Vietnam grew to over 50,000 including 10,000 from the Air Force. Two months later on 25 July the President approved an increase in troop-levels to 125,000 men. As the American ground forces increased, so did US air power.

On 3 May, Marine Observation Squadron VMO-2 flew six new armed UH-1E helicopters into Da Nang and began to take over the role of escorting Marine H-34 troop-carrying helicopters from the Army. The UH-1Es were armed with TK-2 Ground Fire Suppression Armament Kits consisting of an electrically fired M-60C machine gun on each side of the helicopter and two 2.75-inch rocket pods. Also, beginning in April 1967 the UH-1Es were modified to incorporate the Emerson Electric TAT-101 rotating turret below the nose of the aircraft. The turrets contained two M-60 machine guns and were used until April 1972 when more suitable armament became available. One month after the arrival of the UH-1Es HMM-161 became the third Marine H-34 squad-

ron in Vietnam, when it moved into the Phu Bai area near the old imperial city of Hue.

The Marines, whose Phantoms were now flying combat missions out of Da Nang, decided to bring in additional ground support aircraft in the shape of the A-4E Skyhawk. Since only Da Nang, Bien Hoa and Tan Son Nhut were capable of taking jets at that time the Marines decided to build a dedicated attack aircraft facility of their own. On 7 May, 1400 more Marines and Navy Seabees waded ashore at Chu Lai, 50 miles south of Da Nang and began to build an airfield. Using two foot by 12 foot sections of aluminum matting, a 4000 foot long Short Airfield for Tactical Support (SATS) was quickly put into place and mobile arresting gear was set up to facilitate use of the tailhook capability of the Skyhawk. By 1 June the advance elements of Marine Attack Squadrons VMA-225 and 311 had arrived and within hours Skyhawks from VMA-225 had flown their first combat mission, leaving the airfield with the aid of Jet-Assisted Take-Off (JATO) equipment as the field was without an aircraft carrier-type catapult system until 1967.

On 12 May all air attacks on North Vietnam were halted on the orders of President Johnson. Reconnaissance aircraft were sent out to photograph the lines of communication in the North, to help assess the effects so far of the *Rolling Thunder* campaign. At the same time diplomatic feelers were put out to test Hanoi's reaction to the bombing-halt. Hanoi denounced the bombing halt as 'a worn-out trick of deceit and threat' and carried on as before. Two things were now clear; Hanoi did not feel sufficiently intimidated by *Rolling Thunder* to cease its aggression in the South and in fact would not be, until B-52 bombers were unleashed over Hanoi in December 1972, and secondly it was obvious that America had forgotten the hard-earned lessons of the Korean war, that, to force the communists to negotiate seriously, one must bargain from a position of strength. President Johnson was not yet prepared to use that strength and *Rolling Thunder* resumed on 18 May with further attacks below the 20th parallel.

At this point it is appropriate to describe the decision-making process for determining which targets in North Vietnam would be struck next. The

Commander-in-Chief Pacific, after consultation with his subordinates, would forward to the JCS a list of the targets that they would like to strike during the next *Rolling Thunder* period, which was still usually confined to a one or two week time frame. The JCS would consider the targets and the reasons for attacking them, delete some and add others and pass the list on to the Secretary of Defense. Before the list reached the Secretary, however, it would be reviewed by several layers of civilians from the Secretary's vast organizational staff and by various offices in the State Department. The final decision on what targets were to be authorized, the number of sorties allowed, and in many instances, even the tactics to be used by the pilots, was made at a Tuesday luncheon in the White House attended by the President, the Secretary of State, the Secre-

tary of Defense, Presidential Assistant Walt Rostow and the Presidential Press Secretary. No professional military man, not even the Chairman of the Joint Chiefs of Staff, was allowed to attend these luncheons until late in 1967.

One recommendation that the Secretary of Defense did approve was the use of the giant Boeing B-52 Stratofortress bombers. General Westmoreland had requested their use following the attempt in April to destroy the Viet Cong military headquarter complex at Black Virgin Mountain. Four hundred and forty-three sorties were flown against the complex, which was spread over a wide area, whereas carpet-bombing by B-52s might have achieved better results. The Air Force flew its first B-52 strike of Operation *Arc Light* on 18 June 1965 against a suspected Viet Cong base in Binh Duong prov-

ince, north of Saigon. The Army sent three Special Forces bomb damage assessment teams into the area afterwards, but they found little target damage before enemy snipers drove them out of the area. General Westmoreland was satisfied with the results though and by the end of the year the B-52s were flying 300 sorties each month. Sadly, this first mission suffered a tragedy when two of the B-52s collided en route during aerial refueling. Eight of the twelve crewmen lost their lives as the aircraft plunged in flames into the Pacific. On the same day that the mission occurred the ARVN military took over the government again. Major General Nguyen Van Thieu was installed as President and Nguyen Cao Ky, the VNAF commander, became Premier.

On 17 June the Navy scored the first

ABOVE: An F-105D releases a volley of 2.75 inch rockets on a target in North Vietnam.
RIGHT: A Kaman H-2 Seasprite plane guard hovers nearby as a Skyhawk prepares to launch from the *Enterprise*.

MiG kills of the war when two F-4Bs from Fighter Squadron VF-21 found themselves closing on a flight of four MiG-17s south of Hanoi. The Phantoms fired their Sparrow missiles and were delighted to see two of the MiGs go down in flames. Three days later a propeller-driven A-1H Skyraider from Navy Attack Squadron VA-25 brought down a third MiG-17 by using its superior turning ability to out-maneuver the enemy jet. It was quite an accomplishment, especially as the MiG-17s were usually armed with three 23mm cannon and two underwing packs of eight 55mm air-to-air rockets.

By now the communists were capable of mounting regimental-size operations in many parts of South Vietnam and battalion-size operations almost anywhere. The Viet Cong units were now equipped with modern Chinese and Soviet weapons and were being supplemented by the arrival of North Vietnamese Army regular troops. The South Vietnamese armed forces had been doing badly and it appeared that the war on the ground might be lost before the war in the air had even started. Consequently Washington decided to commit American combat troops to battle.

During July US Army Vietnam headquarters was formed at Long Binh near Saigon to support Army operations in Vietnam. The 1st Infantry Division's 2nd Brigade arrived for combat operations in III Corps and 1st Brigade, 101st Airborne Division arrived for combat in II Corps. The 1st Battalion, Royal Australian Regiment had already arrived in III Corps and they were joined by a New Zealand Army field artillery battery. They were the first Allied combat units to arrive; Thai and Korean combat troops were on the way and soon Royal Australian Air Force Canberra bombers, Caribou transports and UH-1 helicopters would deploy. As overall ground commander

General Westmoreland had to decide how to use his combat troops to best effect. He did not, and never would have, enough men nor the time, to seize and hold areas of the countryside in order to destroy the Viet Cong infrastructure and pacify the villages. It is easy to understand the decision facing the General when one realizes that even at the height of American involvement when over half a million servicemen were in Vietnam, only 80,000 were combat troops, the rest being support and service personnel. 'Search and Destroy' became the name of the game and the US troops were sent out into the countryside to locate the enemy and then destroy him using the superior US firepower. It may have been a good theory at the time, but whereas the North Vietnamese leaders had an unlimited supply of 'cannon fodder' to fill their fighting units, the United States did not. At this stage of the war it was not a problem but later when the US media began to show the war in all its questionable glory and the number of coffins arriving at Stateside airports turned from a trickle to a flood, the American public would demand the return of its sons.

Meanwhile, the war in the air continued with the arrival on *Yankee Station* in July of the aircraft carrier

USS *Independence*. One of the squadrons on board was VA-75, the *Sunday Punchers* who were equipped with the new Grumman A-6 Intruder. The Intruders' primary missions were all-weather and night attacks and they were an impressive addition to the Navy's aircraft inventory. The A-6A could bomb accurately in all weathers with its DIANE weapons delivery system and it could carry up to 15,000-pounds of bombs, second only to the B-52. Later in the war KA-6s would be used as airborne fuel tankers and EA-6s on electronic warfare missions, including radar destruction or suppression.

The Navy had scored the first MiG kills on 17 June 1965 and on 10 July the Air Force decided to get in on the act. A flight of four F-4Cs from the 45th TFS at Ubon decided to try a new tactic while escorting some F-105s on a strike mission. As the Thuds began their bomb run the Phantoms held back and waited for the enemy to appear, as they usually did, when the strike force was most vulnerable. Suddenly they sighted a flight of MiG-17s and rolled into the attack, despatching two of the enemy with their Sidewinder missiles. The

BELOW: A reconnaissance photograph of a North Vietnamese SAM site.

RADAR

BAMBOO MATTING

dogfight highlighted a problem that would plague the Phantom crews throughout the war, that of an inadequate fuel capacity. In this case it caused the two MiG-killers to land at Udorn, which was closer than Ubon, with not enough fuel to go around the block. Two weeks later the enemy evened the score when a SAM missile exploded in a flight of four F-4Cs from the 47th TFS, destroying one and damaging three others. By the end of the year 180 SAM launches had been recorded, resulting in the loss of four more USAF and six US Navy/Marine corps aircraft.

No doubt to the relief of the pilots, an adequate Search and Rescue force was now in place. Three Douglas SC-54 Rescue-masters had arrived at Udorn to operate as airborne command posts until the first HC-130s arrived in December 1965. They replaced the ageing HU-16 Albatross amphibians, which then moved to Da Nang and spent the next two years flying rescue missions in the Gulf of Tonkin. The

RIGHT: An F-4B from Fighter Squadron VF-96 from the USS *Enterprise* on *Dixie Station*, firing rockets at a Viet Cong stronghold.
BELOW: The two F-105 wings had around 110 Thuds between them at Korat and Takhli.

LEFT: 1st Squadron, 9th Cavalry in the An Lao Valley, 1967.
BELOW LEFT: CH-46 Sea Knights from HMM-161.
BELOW RIGHT: An M-60 team from the 101st Airborne.

HH-43B/F helicopters were joined in July by two Sikorsky CH-3Cs on loan from Tactical Air Command. With their extra capacity, longer range and protective armor they helped to bridge the SAR gap until the first purpose-built HH-3E Jolly Green Giants arrived in December. In order to provide escorts for the rescue helicopters over Laos and North Vietnam the A-1Es of the 602nd Air Commando Squadron were moved into Udorn in August. Pilots ejecting 'feet wet' over the Gulf of Tonkin could count on rescue by the Navy's SH-3 and UH-2 helicopters. The Sikorsky SH-3A Sea Kings came from the anti-submarine squadrons aboard the ASW carriers and the smaller Kaman UH-2A/B Seasprites from detachments of the Helicopter Combat Support Squadrons on the carriers and smaller ships of TF.77.

On 11 August the USS Princeton sailed from Long Beach, California with Marine Air Group 36 on board. The Group comprised three UH-34

elements of VMO-2 into the Marble Mountain air facility near Da Nang. As soon as MAG-36 arrived the monsoon rains began and turned Ky Ha into a sea of mud. The Marines at Marble Mountain had to contend with sand in everything and the first things to suffer were the helicopter rotor blades. The UH-1E blades were only lasting 200 flying hours instead of 1000 and a critical shortage soon occurred, not only for the UH-1s, but the UH-34s as well. As the Marine build-up was underway the Viet Cong moved the 3000 men of its 1st Regiment close to Chu Lai, ready to try to overrun the airfield. The Marines decided to preempt the attack and on 18 August they launched three Marine infantry battalions against the Viet Cong. Operation *Starlight* lasted four days, with Phantoms and Skyhawks flying support missions so close to the base that they were releasing their bombs even before they had time to raise their wheels. Fifty Marines were killed, but the Viet Cong lost over 600 in their first major defeat at the hands of the Americans. Two months later the Viet Cong attacked the helicopter base at Marble Mountain, destroying 19 UH-1Es and UH-34s and badly damaging 11 others. The short-age of helicopters worsened, but help was on its way.

On 1 July 1965 the 1st Cavalry Division (Airmobile) was activated, following the extensive testing of the Airmobile Division concept by the 11th Air Assault Division (Test). It comprised the resources of the 11th Air Assault Division and the 2nd Infantry Division; namely 1600 vehicles, 15,800 men and 434 helicopters and aircraft. The Division's advance party arrived at An Khe at the end of August and began to clear the 'golf course', which was to become the world's largest helipad. The *First Team's* helicopters were

capable of performing the missions of troop-lift, gunship support, aerial rocket artillery, medevac, artillery spotting, liaison and air cavalry reconnaissance. The troop-lift role was carried out by the new UH-1D which could carry 13 troops; fire-power was supplied by the UH-1B and from 1966, UH-1C gunships; CH-47A Chinooks could carry troops or freight; CH-54 Tarhe flying cranes were used to haul artillery pieces and recover downed aircraft and the OH-13 was used for observation and reconnaissance duties.

The arrival of the 1st Cavalry Division coincided with an attempt by the communists to cut South Vietnam in two. The attempt began with an attack by 2200 North Vietnamese Army (NVA) troops on the Pleime Special Forces camp in the Central Highlands of II Corps on 18 October. The enemy tried for 10 days to overrun the camp in the face of intense USAF air strikes. A total of 1,500,000 pounds of bombs was dropped on the attackers who broke off the attack as reinforcements fought their way through to the camp. Realizing that three North Vietnamese regiments were in the area, General Westmoreland ordered the 1st Cavalry Division to locate and bring them to battle. The month-long Operation *Silver Bayonet* became known as the Battle of the Ia Drang Valley and resulted in 1800 NVA troops killed against 240 Americans.

Additional fighter squadrons arrived during October when the first of five more F-100 squadrons took up residence at Bien Hoa and Da Nang. RF-4C reconnaissance Phantoms arrived from the 16th TRS at Shaw AFB and moved into the already crowded Tan Son Nhut Air Base. On the 23rd the 450th TFS flew the first dozen Northrop F-5A Freedom Fighters into South Vietnam. They were a part of the *Skoshi Tiger* evaluation program and although they could only carry a small payload, they were relatively easy to maintain and repair. The USAF began to train VNAF pilots on the type in Arizona and

BELOW: Loading 7.62 mm ammunition for the guns of a *Spooky* AC-47 gunship.

ABOVE: Crewmen aboard a Navy SAR H-3 Sea King lower freight onto a destroyer.
RIGHT: *Puff the Magic Dragon* fires in support of troops in contact on the ground.

in 1967 the F-5s were turned over to the VNAF.

As losses to the new SAM missiles began to mount, the Air Force tried to counter the threat by launching *Iron Hand* F-105D SAM suppression flights against the SAM sites. This dangerous job became easier with the arrival in November of the first four two-seater F-100F Wild Weasel aircraft. They were based at Korat RTAFB with the 388th TFW and were equipped with radar homing and warning (RHAW) sets which enabled them to home in on the Fansong radar guidance signals for the SA-2 missiles. Once the SAM site was discovered the F-100 would mark the target with rockets for the bomb-carrying F-105s to destroy. The F-100Fs could also give early warning of an impending SAM firing, thus allowing the aircraft in the area to take evasive action. The F-100s and F-105s did not work well together; the F-100 could not carry enough bombs to mount an effective attack alone, the F-105 was much faster and the F-100's AGM-45 Shrike radar-homing missiles

were not very reliable. In the summer of 1966 the F-100s would be replaced by RHAW equipped F-105 Wild Weasels.

The first Douglas AC-47 gunships belonging to the 4th Air Commando Squadron arrived at Tan Son Nhut toward the end of November and flew their first operational sortie on 15 December. The AC-47s were designed to provide fire support at night for isolated outposts such as Special Forces' camps. They were each equipped with three miniguns based on the renowned Gatling design, with each gun capable of firing 6000 rounds per minute. The AC-47 was also modified to carry

24,000 rounds of ammunition and 45 200,000-candlepower flares, which would be tossed out the open cargo hatch to descend on a small parachute, illuminating the area. The guns were fired through windows on the port side of the aircraft by the pilot, using special sights. The aircraft would be held in a pylon turn to the left in order to maintain the concentration of fire on a given point, and its firepower, especially at night, was impressive. It was nicknamed *Spooky* after its operational callsign and *Puff the Magic Dragon* by those who had witnessed one of its nocturnal displays.

Over in Thailand the 8th TFW, the *Wolfpack*, flew its F-4C Phantoms from George AFB in California to Ubon. They were to provide escort cover for the F-105s and eventually took over both the strike and escort role as the F-105 fleet diminished through attrition. The 366th TFW, the *Gunslingers*, began to arrive at Cam Ranh Bay with their F-4Cs, as did the 12th TFW, although the 366th soon moved on to Da Nang. In November the Air Force also began to camouflage its aircraft with the exception of the O-1 FACs who needed to be seen from the air against the jungle background. Shortly afterward a system was begun of allocating two letter tailcodes to the aircraft according to where they were based.

On 2 December the US Navy's first nuclear-powered aircraft carrier USS *Enterprise* arrived on *Yankee Station* with Air Wing 9 on board. The wing consisted of four A-4C Skyhawk squadrons, two F-4B Phantom squadrons, an RA-5C Vigilante squadron and one of KA-3B Skywarriors for airborne refuelling. There were also detachments of E-1B Tracers for the airborne early warning role; UH-2 Seasprite helicopters for SAR and utility duties; EA-3B Skywarriors for electronic intelligence gathering and RA-3B's for reconnaissance. With the E-2A Hawkeye AEW aircraft, A-1 Skyraiders, A-6 Intruders, F-8 Crusaders and SH-3 Sea King helicopters on the other carriers, all the major types of Navy aircraft which were to operate throughout the war were in place. The only exception was the A-7 Corsair II which would arrive in December 1967.

With separate command and control organizations involved in the planning of Navy and Air Force *Rolling Thunder* missions against North Vietnam, it was decided to divide the North into six areas or route packages. In general the Air Force would attack inland targets while the shorter-range Navy aircraft concentrated on those near the coast. Route Package 1, the area just north of the DMZ, was controlled by MACV, the joint command in South Vietnam, as an extension of the Army battlefield. The Air Force flew most of the missions into this package, but the targets were usually chosen by MACV. Route Packages 2, 3 and 4 were strictly Navy operating areas, into which the Air

LEFT: Ordnance waiting to be loaded on to aircraft aboard the USS *Ranger*.

RIGHT: A Phantom from VF-21 on the *Midway* bombs an enemy position.
BELOW RIGHT: An F-100 begins a strafing run on Viet Cong positions in the Delta.

Force could operate only with Navy permission and under Navy control. Of the remaining two packages, the Air Force controlled the fifth, from the west of Hanoi up the Red River Valley to the Chinese border. The sixth was split, with the Navy controlling the portion that included Haiphong and the Air Force controlling the portion from Hanoi northwestward, and both had certain operating rights over the city of Hanoi itself. It was an operations nightmare which could have been avoided by the appointment of a single commander to ensure the effective employment of all available tactical air power. As if this was not enough, the Johnson administration imposed a 30-mile radius restricted zone and a 10 mile prohibited zone around Hanoi and similar zones of four and 10 miles around Haiphong. This was coupled with a 30-mile buffer zone along the border with China. Permission to strike any of the important targets in these zones had to be obtained from Washington and this was seldom given. F-105 pilots could clearly see the enemy MiGs taking off from Phuc Yen airfield, near Hanoi, but were forbidden to engage them.

As the year came to an end authority was given for a strike against one target only within the restricted area of Haiphong. On 22 December 100 aircraft from the *Enterprise*, *Kitty Hawk* and *Ticonderoga* hit the power station at Uong Bi, 15 miles northeast of the harbor city of Haiphong. It was the first raid on an industrial target, as opposed to bases and support installations and all sections of the complex were hit for the loss of two Skyhawks. Two days later President Johnson ordered a Christmas truce and the bombing ceased for 37 days. While Washington waited in vain for the communists to talk peace, North Vietnam took advantage of the bombing halt to improve its anti-aircraft defenses and disperse its petroleum and lubricants facilities. The first phase of *Rolling Thunder* had clearly been a failure. In the 16 months since August 1964 nearly 57,000 combat sorties had been flown from the 10 aircraft carriers and over 100 aircraft had been lost. A total of 82 men had been killed, captured or were missing and 46 others had been rescued.

4. Rolling Thunder, Airmobility and the Trail

The peak years of the Air War in South East Asia were 1966 to 1968. During that time the United States Armed Forces found themselves fighting not one war but three. The *Rolling Thunder* bombing campaign continued over North Vietnam in the vain hope of persuading the North Vietnamese to discuss peace. United States Air Force and Navy aircraft flew North daily, but the restrictions imposed by the Johnson administration, together with the most powerful air defense system in the world, prevented a successful conclusion to the campaign. In South Vietnam the ARVN troops took a back seat while American combat troops sought to bring Viet Cong and North Vietnamese Army units to battle. Employing the mobility afforded by the Bell UH-1 helicopter, the Americans launched search and destroy operations, 'to pin down the enemy and use their massive fire power and air support to destroy them. After the loss of 4000 helicopters and 58,000 men, it would become clear that while North Vietnam was apparently prepared to continue fighting forever, the American public was not.

No doubt the 'folks back home' would have been equally concerned to discover that their sons and husbands were fighting a secret, undeclared air war over the border in Laos as well. While operation *Barrel Roll* continued to hit targets in the northeast of the country, the *Steel Tiger* campaign against the infiltration routes in the eastern edges of the southern panhandle was split into two, with operations south of the 17th parallel and adjacent to the South Vietnamese border being renamed *Tiger Hound*. By 1966 American aircraft were flying 1000 sorties a month in Laos, and between 1964 and 1970 they were to drop more than 2.2 million tons of bombs onto the infiltration routes of the Ho Chi Minh Trail.

As 1966 began the USAF had 500 aircraft and 21,000 men at seven major bases in South Vietnam. Da Nang, Pleiku, Nha Trang, Cam Ranh Bay, Bin Thuy, Bien Hoa and Tan Son Nhut were all in use, and Phan Rang and Tuy Hoa would open later in the year as work began on Phu Cat Air Base. In Thailand USAF squadrons were present at Ubon, Udorn, Takhli, Korat and Don Muang. U Tapao would open

later in the year while development continued at Nakhon Phanom Air Base. Three aircraft carriers were on *Yankee Station* with one more further south on *Dixie Station* and the number of American combat and support troops in Vietnam had risen to 181,000.

By the time the *Rolling Thunder* campaign began again on 31 January 1966, following a 37 day pause, North Vietnam had built up its anti-aircraft defenses to around 2000 guns at 400 sites. They consisted mainly of 37mm and 57mm weapons, but included a few 85mm and 100mm as well. Fifty-six surface-to-air missile sites had also been pinpointed by reconnaissance flights. The MiG pilots were trying to improve their tactics as were the SAM operators who managed to bring down an RB-

PAGES 92-93: Mustang gunships and empty slicks return to a field site at Tay Vinh.
RIGHT: The Vietnam air war, showing bases and the route packages into which the North was divided.
BELOW: A UH-1D slick from A Company, 229th Assault Helicopter Battalion, departs the LZ with the crew chief firing his M-60.

66C Destroyer near Vinh in February, despite continued jamming and evasive action.

On the ground the troop build-up continued throughout the year, with the number of divisions increasing from three to seven and the brigades from two to four, plus an armored cavalry regiment. The Marines with their two divisions were responsible for the northern part of South Vietnam in I Corps, the Army settled in the two middle regions of II and III Corps and the South Vietnamese took responsibility for IV Corps area in the Mekong Delta. Soon operations such as *Van Buren*, *Paul Revere* and *El Paso II* began, culminating in the multi-brigade operation *Attleboro* in November in Tay Ninh Province, which finished with a Viet Cong and NVA 'body count' of 1106.

On 9 March a Viet Cong force of over 2000 men attacked the Special Forces camp at the southern end of the A Shau Valley, near the Laotian border. They were determined to destroy the camp to enable them to set up a supply and staging area, from which to launch attacks into the I and II Corps areas.

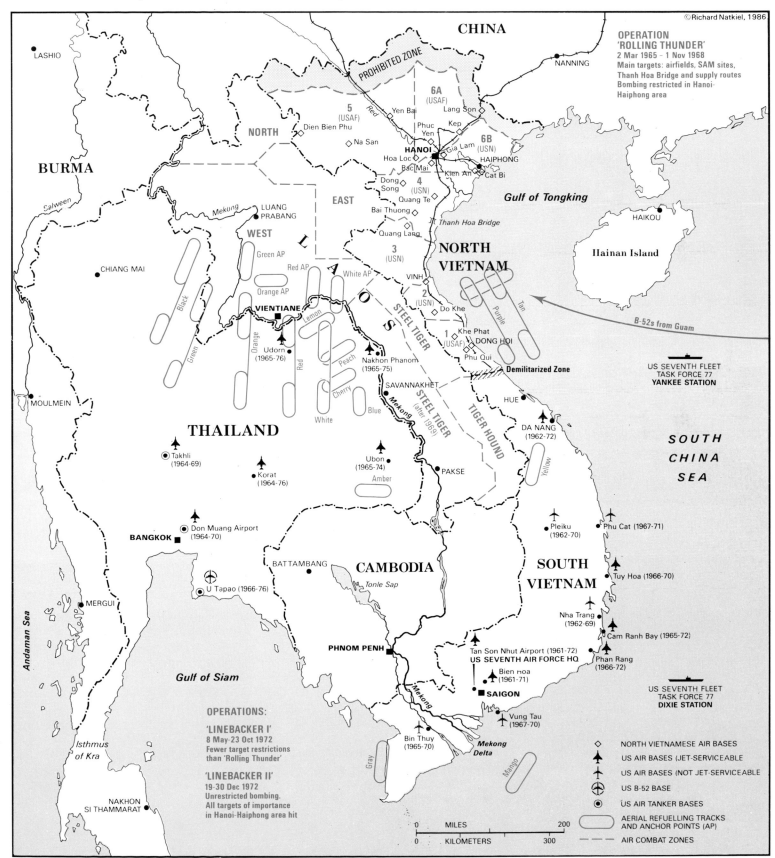

© Richard Natkiel, 1986

OPERATION 'ROLLING THUNDER'
2 Mar 1965 – 1 Nov 1968
Main targets: airfields, SAM sites, Thanh Hoa Bridge and supply routes
Bombing restricted in Hanoi-Haiphong area

OPERATIONS:

'LINEBACKER I'
8 May–23 Oct 1972
Fewer target restrictions than 'Rolling Thunder'

'LINEBACKER II'
19–30 Dec 1972
Unrestricted bombing. All targets of importance in Hanoi-Haiphong area hit

◇ NORTH VIETNAMESE AIR BASES
▲ US AIR BASES (JET-SERVICEABLE
▴ US AIR BASES (NOT JET-SERVICEABLE
⊕ US B-52 BASE
⊙ US AIR TANKER BASES
▭ AERIAL REFUELLING TRACKS AND ANCHOR POINTS (AP)
– – – AIR COMBAT ZONES

MILES 0 — 200
KILOMETERS 0 — 300

The dense cloud cover prevented any air support until the following day when over 200 air strikes were made, killing at least 500 of the attackers. During one of the air strikes Major Wayne Myers of the 1st Air Commando Squadron crash-landed his A-1E Skyraider at the camp's badly damaged airstrip. Seeing his fellow pilot's predicament Major Bernard C Fisher landed his own A-1 and taxied the length of the debris-strewn runway, picked up Myers and took off again through a hail of enemy fire. For his daring rescue Fisher was awarded the Air Force's first Medal of Honor in Southeast Asia. That evening the camp was abandoned and the survivors evacuated by helicopter. Two years would pass before American troops returned to retake the valley.

On the morning of 8 March the weary H-34 and H-37 crews at Marble Mountain looked up to see 27 Boeing-Vertol CH-46A Sea Knight helicopters flying in over the white sand of the beach. They belonged to HMM-165 and were a welcome addition to the Marines' helicopter inventory. With a crew of three, the twin-engined assault and transport helicopter could carry up to 25 troops or 4000 pounds of cargo.

They were joined three months later by HMM-265 with its 24 CH-46As. It soon became apparent, however, that the beautiful white sand of the Vietnamese lowlands was a greater hazard to the CH-46s than the Viet Cong. Sand was being sucked into engines and they had to be replaced after every 300 landings; sand was also finding its way into the fuel system, causing erratic operation. Air and fuel filters were hastily fitted, as were main rotor blades with nickel-plated leading edges, which lasted ten times longer than the original stainless steel ones. It was not long before a number of fatal crashes highlighted structural defects in the CH-46 and the Sea Knight fleet was grounded more than once while modifications took place. Finally, on 29 November 1967 the first of the more powerful CH-46Ds arrived at Phu Bai, north of Da Nang, bringing the total of CH-46s in the 1st Marine Air Wing to 115.

In April B-52D Stratofortresses with the *Big Belly* modification began to replace the B-52Fs on Guam in the Marianas. The modification increased the internal bombload of the B-52D to 60,000 pounds, 22,000 pounds more than the B-52F. They flew their first

ABOVE: An AC-130 *Spectre* gunship opens fire on Viet Cong positions.
RIGHT: A CH-54 Tarhe recovers a damaged CH-47 to the 1st Cavalry base at An Khe.

mission over North Vietnam on 11 April when they struck the Mu Gia pass through which NVA troops and supplies passed on the way to the northern reaches of the Ho Chi Minh Trail. It was the largest bombing raid since World War II and over 600 tons of bombs were dropped. Two months later the Air Force installed the *Combat Skyspot* ground-directed bombing system in South Vietnam. A controller in a ground radar guidance unit would direct the bombers along a designated route to a bomb drop point and signal the release of the bombs at the proper moment.

In the first air battle over North Vietnam since 10 July 1965, F-4Cs shot down two MiG-17s and engaged new MiG-21 fighters for the first time on 23 April. The first USAF kill of a MiG-21 was scored in a battle on 26 April, when one was downed by an AIM-9 Side-winder fired by an F-4C from the 35th TFW at Da Nang.

Seneca • South Carolina 29678

(803) 885-0872

On 13 May 1966 the 53rd Aviation Detachment, Field Evaluation (Provisional) arrived in Vietnam and joined the 147th Aviation Company (Medium Helicopter) at Vung Tau. The 147th was a CH-47 Chinook unit and had arrived in Vietnam in November 1965, following the 1st Cavalry Division's 228th Aviation Battalion, the first Chinook unit to deploy, which had brought its Chinooks over in September 1965. Whereas the normal CH-47 was a medium transport helicopter, significantly larger than the CH-46 and capable of carrying 44 troops, the 53rd had brought with them four Chinook gunships for evaluation. These ACH-47As were armored and armed to the

teeth with rockets, machine guns, cannons and grenade launchers. Over the next two years three of the four were destroyed, one in a most bizarre and tragic accident, when a mounting pin on a 20mm cannon separated during a firing run, causing the gun to elevate and destroy the forward rotor blades. All the crew were killed.

The 1st Aviation Brigade was activated at Tan Son Nhut on 25 May and eventually became one of the largest Army commands in Vietnam. At the height of its involvement it possessed 641 fixed wing aircraft, 441 AH-1G Cobra attack helicopters, 311 CH-47 cargo helicopters, 635 OH-6A observation helicopters and 2202 UH-1 utility

ABOVE: The door gunner on this UH-1B from HAL-3, the *Seawolves*, fires his twin .30 caliber guns at a Viet Cong position.

helicopters. Flying in support of American and Allied forces, the brigade conducted missions as varied as tactical combat assaults, direct fire support, aerial reconnaissance, medical evacuation, and evacuation and relocation of Vietnamese civilians.

On 30 May another attempt to destroy the Thanh Hoa bridge was made using, of all things, a C-130 transport aircraft. Operation *Carolina Moon* involved the use of new mass-focus bombs, which would be dropped into the Song Ma River, float down to the bridge and detonate when sensors in the bomb detected the metal of the bridge structure. The weapons weighed 5000 pounds and resembled large pancakes eight feet in diameter and 2½ feet thick. The design was such that the weapon was detonated initially around its periphery with the resultant force of the explosion focused along the axis of the weapon in both directions. The only problem was that, due to its size, the new weapon could only be carried by a C-130. The first mission went ahead as

planned and five weapons were dropped in the river one mile from the bridge. Fortunately the intense AAA fire missed the C-130 and it returned safely to Da Nang. However, reconnaissance photographs could find no visible damage to the bridge and a second mission was scheduled for the next night. The second C-130 never returned. It was hit by AAA fire and crashed two minutes before the scheduled drop time. There were no survivors and the mass-focus weapon was never used again in Southeast Asia.

Eight Douglas A-26A Invaders arrived at Nakhon Phanom in Thailand on 8 June to take part in Project *Big Eagle*. They were a batch from a group of 50 B-26Ks modified by On-Mark

Engineering and belonged to Detachment 9 of the 1st Air Commando Wing. Equipped with 14 forward-firing 0.50-inch machine guns, a healthy bomb load of 5000 pounds and extra fuel tanks, they began to fly hunter-killer missions against trucks on the Ho Chi Minh Trail. They replaced the older AC-47 gunships and would in turn be succeeded by AC-119 and AC-130 gunships.

In June 1966 General Westmoreland ordered a series of operations aimed at blunting enemy advances into the highlands and neutralizing NVA/Viet Cong food and manpower resources in the coastal regions. The campaign involved Special Forces long-range reconnaissance patrols seeking potential targets,

BELOW: AH-1G Cobra *Patricia Ann* from C Troop, 7th Squadron, 1st Cavalry Regiment hunting for Viet Cong in Tan An Province.

and employment of the fast growing USAF strength, now directed by Westmoreland's new deputy for air, Lieutenant General William W Momyer. Momyer was also commander of the 7th Air Force, which had replaced the 2nd Air Division at Tan Son Nhut in April. One of the successes of the campaign was the defeat of the Viet Cong 9th Division which lost 2000 men throughout the year and was unable to return to combat until the spring of 1967.

From June 1966 onward the *Rolling Thunder* campaign was extended to North Vietnam's vital petroleum storage and distribution system and by the middle of July Navy aircraft had struck the major tank farms at Hanoi, Haiphong and Bac Giang, destroying more than half of the enemy's oil stocks. By this time though, much of the petrol, oil and lubricant (POL) stocks had been dispersed around the countryside and the latter half of the year was spent locating and destroying fuel-laden trucks, railroad cars, barges and smaller storage dumps. At the same time, multi-carrier strikes were aimed at devastating the critical North Vietnamese railyards at Thanh Hoa, Phu Ly, Ninh Binh and Vinh. On 26 October during this intense period of action the carrier force suffered a tragic mishap. A seaman on board USS *Oriskany* improperly handled a flare, which ignited other munitions and set the forward end of the carrier ablaze. It took three hours to extinguish the fire by which time 19 crewmen and 25 naval aviators had died. The ship left the area for repairs and was replaced by the *Coral Sea*.

One Navy unit which operated in an environment totally different to that of the carrier-based fighter squadrons was the HC-1 detachment at Vung Tau. The unit began to fly UH-1B gunships on 19 September in support of US Navy and Army riverine operations in the Mekong Delta. The *Game Warden* Task Force 116, which employed a variety of small boats to patrol the rivers and canals and carry out assault operations against the enemy, welcomed the additional firepower. So successful were the gunships that the unit became a squadron, HAL-3, in April 1967 and over the next five years the gunship strength of the *Seawolves* would rise from eight to 33.

By August 1966 the North Vietnamese air defense system consisted of 271 radars, 4400 anti-aircraft guns and

20-25 battalions of surface-to-air missiles. Their fighter strength was around 65 aircraft including the modern MiG-21 equipped with Atoll air-to-air missiles. In September the MiG force went on the offensive from their five air bases in the Hanoi area which were immune to attack. Confronted by daily MiG-21 challenges the Air Force had to divert F-4Cs from their primary strike role to exclusive aerial combat against the MiGs.

On the ground American strength had increased to 385,300 men by 31 December 1966, together with 735,900 South Vietnamese Armed Forces and 52,500 Allied personnel; 47,712 South Vietnamese and 6644 US military personnel had been killed in action to that date. They were now confronted with an estimated enemy strength in the South of 282,000, including 110,000 NVA regulars.

By the end of 1966 American tactical aircraft had flown 106,500 attack sorties and B-52s another 280 over the North, dropping 165,000 tons of bombs. USAF aircraft losses for the year came to 379 with F-105s suffering the most (126), followed by F-4s (56), A-1s (41), 0-1s (37), F-100s (26), RF-101s (17) and B-57s (13). The majority of the

ABOVE: An Army UH-1D landing supplies on a Navy troop carrier in the Delta.
ABOVE RIGHT: A Russian built MiG-21 Fishbed seen near Hanoi.
RIGHT: A UH-1 lands on the LST *Garrett County*.

losses were caused by AAA and SAMs; only five USAF and four Navy aircraft were lost to MiGs throughout the year. The MiGs paid for their victories though, by losing 23 of their number to US fighters; 17 to USAF and six to Navy crews. MiG-21 hit and run raids increased at the year's end and the first F-105 went down to an Atoll air-to-air missile. The Air Force decided that it was time something was done about the MiGs and as 1967 began the *Wolfpack* prepared to leave its lair.

On 2 January 1967, 56 F-4C Phantoms from the 8th TFW *Wolfpack* roared down the runway at Ubon in Thailand, took off and set a course for North Vietnam. Operation *Bolo* had begun. The task of the *Wolfpack*, led by the legendary Colonel Robin Olds, was to lure the enemy MiG fighters out of the sanctuary of their bases and into combat. They were accompanied by Phantoms from the 366th TFW; F-105

Iron Hand SAM suppression flights from the 355th and 388th TFWs and F-104s, EB-66s and RC-121s, as well as KC-135s in the tanker role.

The Phantoms used F-105 call-signs, altitudes, frequencies and airspeeds to convince the North Vietnamese radar controllers that another F-105 bomber force was inbound. The ruse worked and as the MiG-21s from Phuc Yen Air Base climbed through the clouds they ran head-on into the first flight of Phantoms, led by Olds. During the ensuing melee Olds found himself on the tail of a MiG and threw his Phantom into a violent barrel roll. Closing on the target he fired a Sidewinder missile which veered sharply as it locked-on to the MiG, accelerated and blew it apart. Six more MiG-21s went down that day, followed by another pair two days later. The North Vietnamese had been taught a hard lesson and the skies remained clear of MiGs for the next couple of months.

Following a long bout of inter-service rivalry, the Army transferred all its C-7 Caribou aircraft to the Air Force on 1 January. The Army agreed to relinquish all claims to the operation of fixed-wing tactical airlift aircraft, in

ABOVE: Thanh Hoa bridge attacked by Skyhawks from the *Oriskany* in November 1967.
LEFT: Thai Nguyen thermal plant, following a raid by F-105s in March 1967.

return for a virtual monopoly on the use of the helicopter. Ninety-seven C-7s were handed over in-country and incorporated into the USAF-managed Southeast Asia airlift system. Six additional aircraft were received from Tactical Air Command in February. The two services had other problems to contend with. A shortage of bombs was causing aircraft to fly sorties with only a partial load of ordnance and urgent steps had to be taken to prevent a critical manpower shortage as experienced pilots came to the end of their tours of duty. The Army was particularly hard-hit and many pilots were called back for second tours in Vietnam while the training program strained to keep up with the need for helicopter pilots. By the end of the war 962 Army helicopter pilots and 2005 crewmen had been killed in Southeast Asia.

On the ground General Westmoreland now had seven US divisions, two

ABOVE: A strike on Phuc Yen airfield, a restricted target until October 1967.

paratrooper and two light infantry brigades, one armored cavalry regiment and a reinforced Special Forces group. Two and a half Korean divisions and one mixed Australian-New Zealand force were now in-country and the strength of the South Vietnamese Army stood at 11 divisions of varying quality. Westmoreland planned to use this force to open Highway One, which ran east from Saigon to the coast and then north all the way to the DMZ; campaign along Vietnam's borders; mount operations into War Zone C and D and the *Iron Triangle* around Saigon; force NVA and Main Force Viet Cong units away from populated areas and police the South Vietnamese population. 1967 would be the year of the big battles.

On 22 February 1967 the first American paratroop assault of the war took place during operation *Junction City*, when a battalion from the 173rd Airborne Brigade jumped into War Zone C, a long time Viet Cong stronghold north of Tay Ninh City. The operation

was a follow-up to *Cedar Falls* which had taken place during January in the *Iron Triangle* near Siagon. *Junction City* was carried out on a much larger scale and involved 22 US and four ARVN battalions and a vast number of helicopters, which were used to transport troops into blocking positions and reinforce others in contact with the enemy. The operation terminated in mid-May with 2700 enemy casualties, but had disturbing long-range strategic consequences. The Viet Cong Main Force units now moved their headquarters and supply depots over the border to join their NVA counterparts in Cambodia and Laos, where they were safe from attack. The restrictions of the Johnson Administration applied not only to the air forces in the war, but to those on the ground as well. It was not until 1970 that the first cross-border raids against these sanctuaries were approved and by then it was too late.

President Johnson and his advisers insisted on a four day truce for the Vietnamese Tet religious holiday on 8 February despite the protestations of General Westmoreland, CINCPAC and the Joint Chiefs of Staff. As the

truce began the North Vietnamese started to move 34,000 tons of supplies southward. Again the North Vietnamese were unwilling to talk peace and Admiral Sharp, CINCPAC, urged the release of more targets in the *Rolling Thunder* restricted and prohibited areas. The President only approved a few of the targets, choosing the ones that offered the least risk of counter-escalation. The remaining power plants were included, except those in the center of Hanoi and Haiphong, as were the Haiphong cement plant and the Thai Nguyen steel plant. The Thai Nguyen iron and steel works was the only one in the North capable of making bridge sections, barges and POL drums and it was attacked by F-105s and by F-4Cs on 10 March.

By now new technology had provided the US strike aircraft with the electronic countermeasures (ECM) pod. This had the ability to jam the enemy radar in such a way that the enemy could not determine exact aircraft range and bearing information. To gain maximum radiation coverage from their pods pilots had to fly a specific flight formation position both laterally

power plant in the center of Hanoi was struck, but instead of following up with similar attacks, the outcry from the North Vietnamese Government was so effective that Washington forbade further attacks within 10 miles of Hanoi. Although 85 percent of the enemy's primary electric power capacity had been destroyed, there had only been attacks on 40 percent of his military complexes and 30 percent of his transport targets. He had also figured out which areas were restricted and prohibited and acted accordingly. He moved much of his vital material closer to Hanoi and Haiphong and placed his POL stocks and anti-aircraft sites in populated areas where they were safe.

Throughout the month of May new types of aircraft and helicopters continued to arrive in South Vietnam and Thailand. On the 22nd Marine Heavy Lift Squadron HMH-463 arrived at Marble Mountain with its 22 Sikorsky CH-53A Sea Stallion helicopters. They were reunited with the four CH-53As of their Detachment A who had arrived in January. The Sea Stallion replaced the ageing CH-37 in the helicopter recovery role and was capable of lifting any Marine helicopter in Vietnam. Between January and 22 May, Detachment A had retrieved 103 helicopters, including 72 UH-34s, enough to equip three medium transport squadrons.

The first of the new Cessna O-2B Psy-ops aircraft arrived at Nha Trang on 20 May, equipped with three 600-watt amplifiers and a hand operated leaflet dispenser. The 0-2A FAC models began to arrive at Binh Thuy two weeks later, to act as a stopgap replacement for the venerable 0-1 Bird Dog, until the North American OV-10A arived on the scene. The 0-2 was a twin-boom, two seater observation plane with two engines mounted fore and aft of the cabin. By the end of the war 104 had been lost, compared with 172 0-1s and 63 OV-10s.

By mid-1967 the aircraft with the highest overall loss rate in Southeast Asia was the A-1E Skyraider. The losses per 1000 sorties ranged from 1.0 in South Vietnam, to 2.3 over Laos and up to 6.2 for missions over North Vietnam. The report of a pilot downed usually led to the immediate despatch of an H-3 SAR helicopter, escorted by two *Sandy* A-1Es. Although they were ideal

and vertically. The radar jamming capabilities of the ECM pod caused the North Vietnamese to begin inaccurate barrage firing with SAMs and AAA and gave the US aircraft some freedom within the North Vietnamese SAM environment.

The MiGs still remained a problem and finally the restriction on attacking enemy airfields was temporarily lifted. On 24 April 1967 Navy and Air Force aircraft struck the airfields at Kep, Hoa Lac and Kien An, destroying a score of MiG's on the ground. In August another MiG deterrent would arrive in the shape of the EC-121M *Rivet Top* aircraft, which could detect a MiG taking off and report its position to US aircraft in the area.

In the South, 2 Squadron Royal Australian Air Force deployed to Phan

Rang Air Base and flew its first combat sorties on 23 April. They were equipped with Canberra light bombers and used the call sign *Magpie*. They were one of the most combat effective units in South Vietnam and flew sorties for over three years before losing their first Canberra.

The 19th Fighter Squadron (Commando) at Bien Hoa transferred its 18 Northrop F-5A aircraft to the VNAF 522nd Fighter Squadron on 17 April. By June the first jet aircraft squadron in the VNAF was operational. Eventually the VNAF possessed eight such squadrons, using F-5As, RF-5As, two seater F-5Bs and the more powerful F-5E Tiger IIs, most of which were destined to be captured by the North Vietnamese in 1975.

On 9 May the vitally important

escorts for the slow-moving helicopter, the Skyraiders were extremely vulnerable to the sophisticated enemy anti-aircraft defenses. Of the 25 A-1s shot down over the North between June 1966 and June 1967, seven were lost on rescue missions.

During the month of May, 16 MiG-17s and five MiG-21s were shot down over North Vietnam. Eight were credited to the 366th TFW, five to the 355th TFW, one to the 388th TFW and the remaining seven to the 8th TFW including three claimed by the commander of the *Wolfpack* Colonel Robin Olds. The first of the new F-4Ds joined the 555th TFS at Ubon RTAFB on 28 May. Although they could launch the AGM-62 TV-guided *Walleye* missile against ground targets they were still not equipped with guns for aerial combat. Fortunately the SUU-16A gun pod with its 20mm M61 cannon now began to arrive in the theater, with the first going to the *Gunfighters* of the 366th TFW at Da Nang. In July, 20 more F-4Ds arrived at Ubon to replace the

F-104s of the 435th TFS. One of their F-104s had become the first in the world to acquire 3000 hours of flying time after a mission over North Vietnam on 9 June.

Commando Sabre, the use of two seat F-100F Super Sabres as high-speed FAC aircraft, was initiated on 28 June. Using the call-sign *Misty*, they operated in high threat areas where normal FAC aircraft could not survive. One month later the first two-seat Cessna A-37A Dragonfly light strike aircraft arrived in Vietnam. The 25 aircraft of the *Combat Dragon* deployment were flown by the 604th Air Commando Squadron and joined the 3rd TFW at Bien Hoa.

July 1967 saw a number of tragedies occur, starting on the 7th when two B-52s collided in flight 65 miles southeast of Saigon. Among the casualties was Major General William J Crumm, commander of the Strategic Air Command's 3rd Air Division at Andersen AFB, Guam. Da Nang Air Base suffered an enemy rocket attack on the 15th which killed eight men and wounded 138 others. Heavy damage was inflicted on the bomb storage area and 11 aircraft were destroyed and 31 damaged. Earlier the MSQ-77 *Combat*

Skyspot site at Dong Ha had been destroyed.

The aircraft carrier *Forrestal* arrived on *Yankee Station* on 25 July, on her first combat deployment. On board was Air Wing 17 comprising two F-4B and two A-4E squadrons, one RA-5C Vigilante squadron, plus detachments of KA-3B Skywarriors and E-2A Hawkeyes. A revised *Rolling Thunder* target list had just been approved, permitting attacks on 16 additional fixed targets and 23 road, rail and waterway segments inside the restricted Hanoi-Haiphong area. The carrier began operations immediately and flew 150 sorties over the next four days, without loss. However, just before 11.00 hours on the 29th, as a second launch was being prepared, a Zuni rocket was accidentally fired from an F-4 at the aft end of the flight deck. The rocket struck an A-4's fuel tank which exploded, spreading flames over half of the flight deck. As aircraft and ordnance caught fire and blew up, the flames engulfed the aft end of the ship, trapping crewmen in the berthing spaces below the flight deck. Escort vessels closed on the carrier to spray water onto the flight deck as crewmen pulled bombs off

BELOW: Crewmen on the USS *Forrestal* fight the fire on 29 July 1967.

ABOVE: An EKA-3B Skywarrior from VAW-31 aboard the *Bon Homme Richard*.

aircraft and heaved them over the side. Within an hour the fire on the flight deck was under control, but secondary fires below decks took another 12 hours to contain. One hundred and thirty four men had lost their lives and 21 aircraft were destroyed and 43 others damaged. The *Forrestal* left the area and arrived back at Norfolk, Virginia, for repairs on 14 September.

The July *Rolling Thunder* target list was not of great significance, considering that it contained only 16 of the 274 lucrative targets in the Hanoi/Haiphong Restricted areas and none in the Prohibited areas. It did however, include the Paul Doumer Bridge on the outskirts of Hanoi. At 5532 feet long, the 19-span bridge crossing the Red River was the longest in Vietnam. It carried two highways and a rail track and all the supplies coming into Hanoi passed over it. On 11 August 36 F-105Ds from the 355th and 388th TFWs attacked the bridge with 3000-pound bombs. As Phantoms from the 8th TFW flew MiG CAP over the strike force and dropped bombs on the AAA emplacements, Wild Weasel F-105s engaged the SAM sites. Only two of the strike force Thunderchiefs were damaged and as

they headed for home one railway and two highway spans lay in the river. Seven weeks later the bridge was in use again, but after further raids in October and December the enemy gave up repairing it and built a pontoon replacement to carry rail traffic five miles away.

With the Paul Doumer bridge under repair and 26 trains scheduled each day, the North Vietnamese began to ferry freight cars across the river. One dark night in October an A-6 Intruder from the aircraft carrier *Constellation* was sent to destroy the rail ferry loading slip. Carrying 18 500-pound bombs, the Intruder evaded 16 SAM missiles on the way in, dived down to rooftop height, found the ferry slip in the darkness and dropped its bomb load directly on it. Admiral Sharp, the C-in-C Pacific, fully realized the value of the A-6s all-weather capability; whereas most fighter-bomber aircraft were designed to attack targets that the pilot had to acquire visually, the A-6 has a radar system that allows the pilot to attack a target using radar alone, whether he can see it or not. Admiral Sharp recommended that a minimum of 30 should be deployed aboard the

carriers in the Gulf of Tonkin, and they proved very useful over the North where the weather varied daily from fair to foul. By the end of the war 51 had been lost to enemy action, including two destroyed on 21 August by Chinese Shenyang J-6s (MiG-19s) after they strayed into Chinese airspace.

On 14 September 1967 the first two Sikorsky HH-53B Super Jolly Green Giant helicopters arrived at Vung Tau in South Vietnam. They soon joined Detachment 2, 37th Aerospace Rescue and Recovery Squadron at Udorn RTAFB and represented almost as much of an improvement over the HH-3E as that had been over the HH-43F. The HH-53B had two General Electric T64-3 turboshaft engines, producing 3080 horsepower and on one occasion an HH-53B lifted an A-1E weighing 12,000 pounds and carried it 56 miles from the central Laotian panhandle to Nakhon Phanom. Six additional HH-53Bs reached Southeast Asia before the HH-53C, the ultimate rescue helicopter, arrived in September 1969. Both models were capable of inflight refuelling, had excellent range, improved armor protection in vital areas and three GAU-2B/A miniguns each capable of firing 4000 rounds per minute. The HU-16B Albatross flew its last SAR mission in the same month that the HH-53Bs arrived. During its five years in Southeast Asia four HU-16s had been lost, together with nine crew members. On the credit side they had rescued 47 Navy and Air Force aircrew. Soon the first HC-130P aircraft would arrive to replace the HC-130Hs of the 39th ARRS in the *Crown* (later *King*) airborne mission control role. The HC-130P was a modified HC-130H and was equipped with internal fuel tanks, pumps and drogues to enable it to refuel HH-3 and HH-53 helicopters in the air.

Another version of the C-130 was the AC-130 Gunship II, nicknamed the *Spectre*. Planned as a successor to the AC-47 *Spooky* and later joined by the AC-119G *Shadow* and AC-119K *Stinger*, the first test AC-130 arrived at Nha Trang on 20 September. A week later the *Spectre* flew its first mission,

BELOW: An HC-130H airborne command post of the ARRS at Da Nang in August 1968.

supporting troops in contact at a fire-base in South Vietnam. In November 1967 the AC-130 was cleared to fly armed reconnaissance missions over Laos and proved so successful in the truck-hunting role that a contract was issued to modify seven early JC-130As into gunships. The prototype AC-130 was equipped with four 20mm GE M-61 Gatling cannon and four 7.62mm GE MXU-470 miniguns, together with a Night Observation Device (NOD) or starlite scope, a primitive infrared sensor, a 20 kilowatt searchlight and a 'bread-board' computer to solve the 'Kentucky windage' problems by co-ordinating all the variables involved in a side-firing weapon. Eventually the AC-130 would evolve into the most powerful, sophisticated gunship ever built.

During September 1967 the VNAF began to receive other types of aircraft in the shape of a squadron of C-119 transports. Later they would receive 18 AC-47 gunships as the USAF converted to more modern types. Eventually they would possess two squadrons of AC-119s and one of AC-47s. The Bell UH-1 Huey began to replace the ageing H-34 helicopters and as the US began to withdraw from Vietnam other types would join the Vietnamese Air Force

inventory, such as the C-7 Caribou, C-123 Provider, C-130 Hercules and CH-47 Chinook.

USAF combat sorties in South Vietnam exceeded the one million mark in September 1967. By 16 October there were 1500 aircraft deployed to Southeast Asia and three days later the total aircraft losses passed the 1000 mark. Back in the United States, opposition to the war had increased and on 21 October 50,000 anti-war demonstrators marched on the Pentagon. The Preparedness Subcommittee of the Senate Armed Services Committee had conducted extensive hearings in August, into the conduct of the air war against North Vietnam. Secretary McNamara, who would resign at the end of the year, defended the Administration's policy of gradual escalation. Top military leaders involved in the *Rolling Thunder* campaign, including Admiral Sharp (CINCPAC), put forward their arguments for an escalation of the campaign and their opinions were largely endorsed by the committee.

President Johnson took the hint and approved an attack on North Vietnam's third port at Cam Pha on 10 September. MiG opposition increased through October and on the 24th a strike against

LEFT: The Control and Reporting Centre at Monkey Mountain near Da Nang was a part of the *College Eye* EC-121 network.

designed to detect enemy movements on the Trail. The programme was given a succession of nicknames including *Muscle Shoals*, *Mud River* and *Dump Truck*, but *Igloo White* was the best known and used the longest. Strings of seismic and acoustic sensors were air-dropped in designated jungle areas, where they would pick up the sounds and movements of enemy vehicles and personnel, and transmit automatically to orbiting aircraft, such as EC-121s and Beechcraft QU-22 Bonanzas. The aircraft would relay the information back to the Infiltration Surveillance Center, known as the *Dutch Mill* because of the unique shape of its antenna, at Nakhon Phanom RTAFB. The Center's computers would interpret the signals and produce information on the volume of traffic, convoy speed and hours of operation. Interdiction aircraft would then be sent to that area to fix and destroy the supply trucks or infiltrating troops.

In November the first modified Lockheed OP-2E Neptunes from Navy Observation Squadron V0-67 arrived at Nakhon Phanom RTAFB. They wore dark jungle green camouflage and were to be used to drop the sensors along the Ho Chi Minh Trail. Unfortunately the slow-moving Neptunes were easy meat for the enemy anti-aircraft gunners and before long three had been lost. The unit was disestablished in July 1968 and its role was taken over by the F-4s of the 25th TFS.

On the ground the big battles of 1967 had brought the number of US troops killed so far to over 16,000. These included very heavy losses incurred by the 4th Infantry Division and the 173rd Airborne Brigade in the Battle of Dak To. Dak To was in Kontum Province in the Central Highlands and the opening rounds in the battle were fired in June 1967 when the US Special Forces camp was attacked and two battalions of the 173rd Airborne Brigade were airlifted in. On the 22nd one of the companies clashed with a battalion of North Vietnamese troops in one of the most violent battles of the war. Seventy-six paratroopers were killed that day and as losses mounted the 101st Airborne Division in Kentucky was ordered to provide 450 replacements to the 173rd, despite the fact that the 101st was re-

Phuc Yen air base was finally approved. The following day a joint Navy and Air Force raid destroyed nine MiGs on the ground and rendered the base unserviceable. Air strikes continued against every jet-capable airfield in North Vietnam, except Hanoi's international Gia Lam airport. Many of the MiGs were dispersed to bases in China, while repairs were made to their own airfields and their MiG losses made up with replacements. Earlier in the month President Johnson had asked the Joint Chiefs of Staff what could be done to put more pressure on Hanoi. They proposed a ten point list of suggestions, including the removal of all restrictions

on significant military targets, the mining of North Vietnamese ports and waterways, and the expansion of operations into Laos and Cambodia. The JCS would not have many more chances to try to change the President's strategy into one which might have succeeded. However, their ten recommendations were rejected and five months later, in March 1968, US de-escalation began.

In the meantime, US air operations continued over Laos in an attempt to stem the flow of men and supplies down the Ho Chi Minh Trail to South Vietnam. A rudimentary, air supported, electronic anti-infiltration system came into being toward the end of 1967,

organizing as the second airmobile division. More reinforcements arrived including ARVN infantry and paratroopers, and elements of the 1st Cavalry Division and the 4th Infantry Division. The next few months were spent in gruelling marches into the western depths of Kontum Province where the NVA were firmly entrenched in bunker complexes. In November an enemy mortar attack on Dak To airfield set off the ammunition dump and destroyed two C-130 cargo aircraft. On the 18th the fight for Hill 875 began and became the climax of the Battle of Dak To and the 1967 campaign for the Highlands. The fanatical 174th NVA Regiment held the hill and decimated the attack-

LEFT: The capture of a USAF pilot staged for the cameras by the North Vietnamese.
BELOW: An F-8E Crusader from VF-211 at the point of recovery on the *Bon Homme Richard*.

ing Americans. A misplaced bomb from an Air Force airstrike killed or badly wounded 50 paratroopers and the 335th Aviation Company had six of its helicopters shot down as they brought in reinforcements. On the 21st the Air Force dropped seven and one half tons of napalm on the NVA defenders and continued their airstrikes throughout the whole of the 22nd. The next morning the paratroopers reached the summit of the hill, abandoned by the broken 174th Regiment. The battle had involved 2096 tactical air sorties, 257 B-52 bombing strikes and the Chinooks of the 179th Aviation Company later recovered the carcasses of over 40 downed helicopters.

The aircraft carrier *Ranger* arrived on *Yankee Station* on 3 December, with the new Vought A-7A Corsair II on board. They belonged to VA-147, the first operational Corsair squadron and flew their first combat mission on the 4th. By now the monsoon season had begun in the North and the bad flying conditions caused a reduction in combat sorties, with only the A-6s flying on a regular basis. The enemy AAA defences claimed the first A-7A to ground-fire on 22 December and the SAM threat was

renewed as the North Vietnamese began installing optical tracking devices on their SAM guidance systems, severely degrading the effectiveness of the ECM pods.

During the year the USAF lost 421 aircraft in Southeast Asia, including 113 F-105s and 95 F-4s. The enemy had launched 16 attacks on air bases throughout the year and destroyed or damaged 81 aircraft on the ground. The USAF had flown 878,771 combat sorties, an increase of 69 percent over 1966; 681,000 tons of munitions had been expended, or 87 percent more than in 1966; 485,000 US military personnel were now in Vietnam and the war appeared to be going well – or so they thought.

On 21 January 1968 the North Vietnamese unleashed a heavy mortar, artillery and rocket attack on the Marines' base at Khe Sanh and began assaulting outlying defenses west of it. The base was located on a plateau in the northwestern corner of I Corps and commanded the approaches to Dong Ha and Quang Tri City from the west and the coastal corridor leading to Hue. By capturing this important strategic outpost the North Vietnamese would

have an almost unobstructed invasion route in the northernmost provinces, from where they could outflank American positions south of the DMZ. General Giap also hoped to emulate his great Viet Minh victory over the French at Dien Bien Phu 14 years earlier. This time though, things would be different; the French had been short of tactical air support but the Americans had plenty standing by.

Operation *Niagara* began with an average of 300 tactical sorties each day, including, at the height of the battle, the arrival of three B-52s every 90 minutes. Resupply was not easy though, as the lumbering C-123 and C-130 transport aircraft were easy targets for the enemy gunners. One C-123 was shot down, killing all 48 personnel on board and a Marine KC-130 carrying fuel was hit and crashed, with only two survivors. Over a two and one half month period

more than 24,000 tactical and 2700 B-52 sorties dropped 110,000 tons of ordnance in defense of the base. On 1 April, as the weather improved, Operation *Pegasus* was begun, to relieve the

besieged base, but by then the enemy had had enough and withdrew.

Nine days after the siege of Khe Sanh began the Tet celebration of the lunar new year started. It was South Viet-

LEFT: UH-1Ds depart after landing members of the 1st ARVN Division in the A Shau Valley.
RIGHT: By January 1968 the in-country C-130 strength had risen to 72 aircraft.
BELOW: Troops running from UH-1D slicks of the 229th Assault Helicopter Battalion at an LZ near Bong Son.

nam's biggest annual holiday, a time when debts would be paid and feasts served as families and friends gathered. For over a week all business and Government would stop. President Thieu left Saigon to spend the holiday with relatives in the Mekong Delta and almost half of the 732,000 strong armed forces went on leave.

On 30 January, as a 36 hour Tet cease-fire supposedly went into operation, all hell broke loose. Viet Cong and North Vietnamese forces attacked nearly every important city, provincial capital and military installation in South Vietnam. Even the American Embassy in Saigon was attacked, by a

LEFT: Troops waiting for pick-up at an LZ in a heavily defoliated area near Tay Ninh.
BELOW: An HH-3E from the 37th ARRS with an escort of two *Sandy* A-1s from the 6th SOS.

suicide squad of 15 Viet Cong sappers who breached the walls but failed to gain entry to the Chancery. Nearly 700 enemy troops attacked Tan Son Nhut Air Base and the adjoining MACV compound, housing General Westmoreland's headquarters and the 7th Air Force Command Center. As MACV staff officers grabbed weapons and ran outside to help sand-bag the compound, UH-1 gunships from the 120th Assault Helicopter Company *Razorbacks* roared in to attack the enemy breaching the base perimeter.

Two battalions of Viet Cong and NVA troops attacked Bien Hoa Air Base and soon dozens had fought their way through the perimeter into the base. Unfortunately for them, the base was playing host to the Bell AH-1G Cobra gunship New Equipment Training Team (NETT) which had arrived with the first six Cobras four months before. The new gunship was a vast improvement over the armed UH-1s; with a frontal area only three feet wide and a crew of two seated in tandem, it presented a much smaller target to enemy gunners. It was armed with a revolving turret under the nose, equipped with a Minigun and 40mm grenade launcher and could carry a variety of gun and rocket pods on short wing stubs behind the cockpit. The 334th Assault Helicopter Company had begun to convert to the new gunship and when the enemy attack began they took to the air with a vengeance. The communist losses were tremendous with 139 killed at the base and a further 1164 in the surrounding area.

United States and South Vietnamese forces regained control quite rapidly, although the extent of the Tet Offensive had clearly caught them by surprise. The communists captured part of the city of Hue, including the Citadel, and held on for a month, during which time they slaughtered over 3000 innocent civilians. By the time they had been driven from the city, much of the ancient capital of Vietnam had been destroyed.

The Tet Offensive had been well planned and was designed to destroy both the administrative structure and the political base of the South Vietnamese Government. The communists also expected their attacks to initiate a general uprising against the Govern-

RIGHT: A relieved Navy flier, Lt Ronald Ball, being plucked from the sea by an SH-3A.

ment and cause large scale defections from the South Vietnamese Army. These aims were thwarted though, and a large number of Viet Cong and North Vietnamese troops were killed, because for the first time they had come out into the open where the superior US firepower could be brought to bear. In just two weeks, from 29 January to 11 February the communists lost 32,000 killed and 5800 captured, close to half the number of troops actively committed. US forces lost 1001 killed and South Vietnamese and Allied losses were put at 2082. The greatest effect of the Tet Offensive was felt, however, not in Vietnam, but in Washington.

The siege of Khe Sanh and the Tet Offensive sent the Washington Administration into a state of shock. Hanoi had taken a big gamble and had lost on the battlefield, but they had won a psychological victory in the USA. The American public now began to voice its dissatisfaction with the war.

The opinions of the media and antiwar protesters not withstanding, the United States was now in an excellent position to win the war in South Vietnam. The Viet Cong and North Vietnamese forces in the South had suffered huge losses during the Tet Offensive and it would take time to restore their pre-Tet man-power and supply levels. Now was the time to abolish the prohibited zones around Hanoi and Haiphong and along the border with China. The major ports and harbors could have been mined to cut off outside support to the North and a major air campaign without restrictions could have destroyed the warmaking capability of North Vietnam and punished it sufficiently to force it to halt its insurgency in the South.

The civilian leaders in Washington however saw things differently. The biased and often misleading media coverage of the siege at Khe Sanh and the Tet Offensive had increased public pressure on the Johnson Administration to end the war. To give General Westmoreland the number of troops he really required would have meant mobilization and after all, it was an election year.

TOP LEFT: Ordnancemen on the *Kitty Hawk* roll 500-pound bombs across the deck.
LEFT: Setting the fuses on the bombs on an A-6A on the *America*.
RIGHT: A Navy door gunner loading 7.62mm rounds and M-79 grenades into his gunship.

The President and his advisers yet again turned a deaf ear to the advice of the Joint Chiefs of Staff. On 31 March, President Johnson announced that, in an attempt to persuade the North Vietnamese to begin peace negotiations, all bombing north of the 20th parallel was to cease forthwith. Toward the end of his speech, the President also announced that he would neither seek, nor accept, the nomination of his party for another term as President of the

LEFT: *Combat Lancer* F-111As over the Pacific en-route to Thailand.
BOTTOM LEFT: Two heavily laden A-6A Intruders of VA-196 from the *Constellation*.
BELOW: The ground proximity extraction system is used to pull a pallet of supplies from a C-130 at Khe Sanh.

United States. Shortly after the *Rolling Thunder* operations north of the 20th parallel were halted, the US media denounced a naval air raid on transportation facilities near Thanh Hoa, an important communications and traffic center just south of the 20 degree line. In order to appease the media the demarcation line was lowered still further to the 19th parallel.

President Johnson's speech of 31 March marked a major turning point in the war. American policy was now committed to a negotiated, as opposed to a military settlement of the war and this new policy began with major concessions to the enemy. The North Vietnamese response to the limiting of the bombing campaign to the relatively target-free area just north of the DMZ,

was to increase the amount of supplies flowing south; improve its anti-aircraft defenses and start to infiltrate 75,000 replacement troops down the Trail.

Two weeks before President Johnson's speech on the war, on 15 March, six General Dynamics F-111A swing-wing fighter-bombers arrived at Takhli RTAFB. They were Detachment 1 of the 428th TFS from the 474th TFW at Nellis AFB in Nevada and their deployment went by the name of *Combat Lancer*. The F-111 was equipped with terrain following radar which would enable it to deliver a full load of 24 500-pound bombs on any target, in any weather, by flying undetected under enemy radar. Sadly three of the *Combat Lancer* aircraft were lost within a month and the detachment returned home by

ABOVE: A VNAF C-123 Provider fitted with defoliation equipment.
RIGHT: An F-4B Phantom from VF-142 flying a combat air patrol.
FAR RIGHT: C Troop, 3rd Squadron, 17th Cavalry Regiment were one of the many users of the OH-6 Loach.

the end of the year. At least two of the losses were caused by tailplane failure due to fatigue at a welding joint, and this, and other problems, prevented the return of the F-111 to Southeast Asia until September 1972.

United States forces returned to the A Shau valley during operation *Delaware* on 19 April. Since March 1966, the North Vietnamese had used the area as a supply and staging base for attacks into I and II Corps and had constructed elaborate defenses and anti-aircraft sites around the valley. The 1st Cavalry and 101st Airborne Divisions carried out a major airmobile assault in the northern end of the valley while the 1st ARVN Division approached from the east. The weather was unbelievably bad and the anti-aircraft fire so intense that by the time the operation was terminated on 17 May the 1st Cavalry Division alone had lost 21 helicopters. The operation was a success in the short term, because the enemy put up a fight and then retreated

ABOVE: Men of the 9th Cavalry deploy from a UH-1D during Operation *Oregon*, April 1967.
LEFT: North Vietnamese troops examine the wreckage of an American aircraft.

over the border, abandoning a mountain of supplies. Nine hundred communists were killed against 100 Allied dead and 1,000,000 rounds of ammunition and 3000 individual weapons were captured. In 1969 though, the NVA would choose to fight and it would be a different story.

By 1968 the helicopter observation and reconnaissance role had been taken over by the Hughes OH-6A Cayuse. It replaced the old Bell OH-13 Sioux and Hiller OH-23 Raven, which had suffered losses of 170 and 95 respectively by the war's end. The OH-6A Loach as it became known, saw extensive action with the air cavalry troops, usually

ABOVE: Visitors to a North Vietnamese SAM site examine an SA-2 Guideline missile.
RIGHT: The control point of an anti-aircraft defense unit near Hanoi.

working in a *Pink Team* with an AH-1G Cobra gunship. Flying as armed aero scouts, the Loaches were usually the first to engage the enemy, a fact reflected in their total war losses of 955, with 658 of those lost in combat.

North Korean gunboats had seized the USS *Pueblo* in the Sea of Japan off Korea on 24 January and the following day President Johnson ordered the mobilization of 11 Air National Guard squadrons. Two of the squadrons were sent to South Korea and four others were deployed with their F-100C Super Sabres to South Vietnam. The 120th TFS, Colorado Air National Guard (ANG) arrived first on 5 May and joined

ABOVE: With his head bandaged and uniform in shreds Lt Colonel James Lindberg-Hughes is led to a press conference in Hanoi.

the 35th TFW at Phan Rang Air Base. The 174th TFS, Iowa ANG arrived next and joined the 37th TFW at Phu Cat Air Base. Lastly the 136th TFS, New York ANG and 188th TFS, New Mexico ANG arrived to join the 31st TFW at Tuy Hoa Air Base. All four squadrons flew combat missions until returning home in 1969. Five pilots and 14 aircraft failed to return.

The immediate post-Tet period saw a number of changes occur among the American war-managers. Secretary of Defense McNamara had been replaced by Clark M Clifford on 1 March. General Westmoreland was promoted to Chief of Staff of the Army on 10 June and replaced by General Creighton W Abrams. The new General would bring far-reaching changes to the battlefront, mainly in an effort to reduce US combat losses and to involve the South Vietna-

mese Army more, in what was after all, their war. A month later on 31 July Admiral Sharp retired as Commander-in-Chief Pacific and was replaced by Admiral John S McCain.

The combat base at Khe Sanh had been dismantled and abandoned by 23 June. Despite the vast expenditure of munitions and supplies in support of the besieged Marines in February and March, the base had outlived its usefulness. On the 28th the 101st Airborne Division became the Army's second airmobile unit. The reorganization was to take a year to complete, due to the shortage of helicopters and the need to continue combat operations throughout the conversion period.

The first of the new twin-turboprop OV-10A Bronco aircraft arrived at Da Nang on 6 July. They were used by the Marines of VMO-2 at Marble Mountain

and later by VMO-6, to take over the role of the UH-1E armed helicopter in conjunction with the AH-1G Cobra, which the Marines would receive in April 1969. The Bronco could be armed with a 3600-pound weapons load of guns, bombs and rockets and by the end of July 1968 the USAF had also received their first OV-10 to be used in the forward air controller role. The USAF OV-10 FACs were used extensively over South Vietnam and Laos and were particularly useful over the Ho Chi Minh Trail, where their laser designators could pinpoint targets at night, for fighters carrying laser-guided bombs.

During the night of 26 July, Udorn RTAFB was attacked by a small force of communist sappers using explosive charges and small arms. This was the first such attack against a base in Thailand and one Thai security guard and a US crewmember were killed and three others wounded. A C-141 Starlifter transport aircraft was severely damaged and an RF-4C and HH-43 lightly damaged.

By the end of July 1968 the USAF, Navy and Marines had dropped around 2,500,000 tons of bombs on North Vietnam; 877 fixed wing aircraft and nine helicopters had been lost over North Vietnam in the process. Over both North and South Vietnam 382 pilots and 289 aircrew had been killed and 702 were listed as missing. Many of the missing were now guests of the North Vietnamese in prisoner of war camps, where beatings and torture were widespread.

On 7 September, the 8th TFW at Ubon RTAFB recorded its 50,000th Southeast Asia combat sortie, with a bombing mission over the southern panhandle of North Vietnam. During the same month *Go Get 'Em*, an F-4D of the 13th TFS at Udorn flew 80 combat sorties over the North, breaking all existing records for the number of sorties flown in a one month period by a Phantom.

RIGHT: The staged capture of a US pilot by North Vietnamese militia.
BELOW: An A-7A Corsair II follows an A-3 from a catapult on the USS *America*.

123

The F-102A interceptor detachment at Bien Hoa Air Base returned home to Clark Air Base on 25 September. This eased the strain on the one interceptor squadron at Clark, which was also responsible for deployments to Thailand and Korea. As they departed, another detachment arrived in the shape of four Lockheed AP-2H Neptune gunships. These modified SP-2Hs were a part of the Trails and Road Interdiction, Multisensor (TRIM) program and were assigned to the Navy's Heavy Attack Squadron VAH-21 at Cam Rahn Bay. They were armed with two forward-firing Minigun pods, two 500-pound bombs and two incendiary bombs mounted under the wings. They also carried a twin 20mm cannon in the tail and were later fitted with a 40mm grenade launcher in the bomb bay. To carry out their night interdiction role,

LEFT: Lt Patton of VA-176 was one of only two pilots to shoot down a MiG with his A-1H.
RIGHT: Colonel Robin Olds of the 8th TFW adds another red victory star to an F-4C.
BELOW: Lt Clyde Lassen, pilot of an HC-7 H-2 Seasprite won the Medal of Honor for a rescue in January 1968.

ABOVE: A USAF Cessna A-37A Dragonfly fires rockets at a Viet Cong target.
TOP LEFT: An A-4E from Attack Squadron VA-144 returns to the *Bon Homme Richard* after a mission.
BOTTOM LEFT: Despite its official task of battlefield reconnaissance, the OV-1 also carried rockets, guns and napalm.

they were equipped with a Forward Looking Infrared (FLIR) and Low Light Television (LLTV) sensor. A Side-Looking Airborne Radar was mounted on both sides of the fuselage and the tail-gunner used a Night Observation Scope in place of the standard reflector gunsight. The anti-submarine warfare radome had been replaced with an AN/APQ-92 search radar and additional equipment included a Real Time IR sensor, an airborne Moving Target Indicator, DIANE (Digital Integrated Attack and Navigation Equipment) and a Black Crow truck ignition sensor. Between September 1968 and June 1969 the four aircraft flew over 200 missions, mostly in the *Parrot's Beak* area of the Mekong Delta, but also in Cambodia and Laos against the Ho Chi Minh Trail. All four returned safely to the United States.

The 18th and last MiG kill credited to a Crusader took place on 19 September when two F-8Cs from VF-111 on the carrier *Intrepid* spotted a pair of MiG-21s and climbed to intercept them. Lieutenant Anthony Nargi maneuvered behind one of the MiGs and fired a Sidewinder missile which blew the entire tail off the enemy fighter as the pilot ejected. A 19th MiG kill was claimed by an F-8 pilot from the *Hancock* in May 1972, but as the enemy pilot ejected before the Crusader got within firing range, the kill was not approved.

Toward the end of the summer, enemy forces operating from sanctuaries in Cambodia, began to increase their attacks in the area north of Saigon.

ABOVE: A North Vietnamese MiG-17 camouflaged in a clearing near Gia Lam.
LEFT: The maintenance area for the Marine F-4s of VMFA-115 and 323 at Da Nang.

As a result the 1st Cavalry Division was ordered to move down to III Corps to reinforce US troops in the area. The entire division was moved by air and sea in only two weeks and by mid-November was conducting operations along the Cambodian border.

On 1 November 1968, following the advice of his negotiating team in Paris, President Johnson ordered a halt to all bombing of North Vietnam. His negotiators naively believed that they had reached an understanding with the North Vietnamese, that substantive talks would begin as soon as the bombing stopped. They were wrong. The communists began to repair the bridges and roads below the 19th parallel, strengthen their anti-aircraft defenses and improve their airfields. Truck movements of supplies to their troops in the South increased four-fold. However, the *Rolling Thunder* campaign was now finished and although the ground war in the South and the air war over Laos would continue, American bombers would not return to the North again until 1972. Four days later, on 5 November, Republican Richard M Nixon defeated Democrat Hubert H Humphrey and became the new President of the United States.

5. Vietnamization

As 1968 came to an end the new President and his team prepared to move in to the White House. President Nixon had come to power with a promise to reduce the US commitment in Vietnam and bring America's sons home. The policy was now one of Vietnamization, in which the forces of South Vietnam would be supplied with arms and logistical support to enable them to face up to the North Vietnamese, while the American combat troops withdrew.

President Nixon was a strong President and despite the civil unrest and public discontent with the war, he was not about to abandon South Vietnam. He would not re-start the *Rolling Thunder* campaign, but during his term of office he did authorize cross-border operations into the enemy sanctuaries in Laos and Cambodia, approve secret bombing raids into Cambodia and when all efforts at finding peace had failed he ordered the mining of the North Vietnamese ports and sent the B-52s against Hanoi.

During the change-over of administrations and while the new Vietnamization policy was being formulated, the air war over South Vietnam and Laos continued. The fighters and bombers which had been so misused in the *Rolling Thunder* campaign were now available for use against the enemy infiltration routes through Laos and Cambodia. An extensive interdiction campaign called *Commando Hunt* was begun in Laos on 15 November. The campaign was concentrated in the *Barrel Roll* and *Steel Tiger* areas and its objectives were to destroy as much as possible of the supplies being moved down the Trail, to tie down enemy manpower and to test further the effectiveness of the sensor system. The campaign drastically increased the number of sorties flown in Southeast Asia from 4764 tactical and 273 B-52 sorties in October, to 12,821 and 661 in November.

It is an unfortunate fact that despite the best efforts of the US Air Force, Navy and Marines, the flow of men and material down the Ho Chi Minh Trail actually increased, rather than decreased, every year. To the pilots flying the missions it must have been like trying to beat a snake to death starting at the tail. They were risking their lives hunting for individual trucks coming down the jungle trails, usually in the dark, whereas it would have been a far more effective use of air power to have sent strikes against the supply bases and ammunition dumps near the ports in North Vietnam, from where the trucks began their journey.

Two new types of aircraft made an appearance over the Trail during November, the RA-3B Skywarrior and the NC-123K Provider. The RA-3Bs were from the Navy's Heavy Photographic Squadron VAP-61 and were equipped with infrared sensors so they

PREVIOUS PAGE: A line-up of VNAF C-47s at Tan Son Nhut Air Base.
BELOW: A Skyhawk from VA-23 on the USS *Oriskany* drops its load of 500-pound bombs.

ABOVE: A Skywarrior returning to the USS *America* about to catch the arrester cable.
RIGHT: The USAF and Marines both used the OV-10 Bronco.

could roam the trails at night, looking for truck traffic. Flying below 500 feet the RA-3Bs sensors could detect hot spots, indicating traffic on the Trail and then orbiting A-4 Skyhawks would be called in to attack the targets. The NC-123Ks were a part of the *Black Spot* program and were modified as night interdiction bombers, rather than gunships. The two NC-123Ks were equipped with Forward Looking Radar in a five foot long nose housing and FLIR, LLTV and a laser illuminator/rangefinder mounted in a sensor turret just aft of the new radome. They were also fitted with weapons release computers and armed with 36 Cluster Bomb Units (CBUs) mounted in dispenser chutes in the aft cargo compartment. Both aircraft underwent further modifications in 1969 and returned to the United States in June 1970.

Gun-equipped Phantoms finally arrived in Southeast Asia on 17 November, when 20 F-4Es flew into Korat RTAFB to join the 469th TFS. The new model retained its Sparrow/Sidewinder capability, but carried a 640 round 20mm Vulcan cannon in its nose. The 469th was unable to test the new

gun in a dogfight though. With the bombing halt over the North in effect, it would be three more years before another MiG would be downed.

One new weapon which could be tested as soon as it arrived was the Fairchild AC-119 Gunship III. The AC-130 was supposed to take over the role of the AC-47, but production delays led to the AC-119 arriving first. Like the AC-47 the AC-119 was built with the Troops In Contact (TIC) support mission in mind. It was armed with four 7.62mm Minigun pods and with its extra ammunition supply it was about 25 percent more effective than the AC-47. The aircraft was fitted with a 20kW Xenon searchlight, a Night Observation Sight, LAU-74A Flare Launcher, General Precision fire control computer and a TRW fire control safety display to ensure that the aircraft did not fire on friendly troops. The first AC-119s of the *Combat Hornet* deployment arrived at Nha Trang on 22 December and were given the call-sign *Shadow*. They belonged to the 71st Special Operations Squadron (SOS) and became part of the 14th Special Operations Wing. All Air Commando Wings and Squadrons had been redesignated Special Operations Wings and Squadrons during the summer. The 14th SOW was unique with its 'one of a kind' squadrons. They had the only AC-47 units in the 3rd and 4th SOS; the only two psywar units in the 5th and 9th SOS; the 20th SOS was the only armed helicopter unit in the Air Force; plus the AC-119G and later, AC-119K squadrons. The Wing had flown 200,000 missions by March 1970.

By the end of 1968 the USAF in Southeast Asia had lost another 392 aircraft; 88 to operational causes, 257 to ground fire, 35 were destroyed in attacks on air bases and a dozen were lost to MiGs and SAMs. The latter figure was down from the 40 lost in 1967 and reflected the decrease in air activity over North Vietnam.

During 1968, 16,511 US military personnel had been killed, the highest number for any year of the war. Another indication of the intensity of the fighting on the ground is the total of the US Army fixed-wing and helicopter

losses for the year. These were up to 1008, one third more than in 1967. Over 42,000 Medevac helicopter sorties were flown during the year and 67,000 people were rescued or evacuated.

January 1969 saw the US forces in Vietnam reach a peak of 365,600 Army personnel and 176,800 from other services. Most of the fighting now would be against regular North Vietnamese Army units, following the decimation of the Viet Cong during the Tet Offensive. The cessation of the bombing campaign over the North now allowed the free movement of supplies all the way from the Haiphong docks to the border with Laos, where they would follow the Trail to the South.

LEFT: A USAF HH-53B recovers a downed crew man, with no apparent enemy opposition.
ABOVE RIGHT: The only Navy unit to use the OV-10 was Light Attack Squadron VAL-4.
RIGHT: A downed US pilot grabs for the collar lowered by the rescue helicopter.

ABOVE: An AC-119G *Shadow* gunship from the 71st SOS orbiting near Nha Trang.
LEFT: Two pictures of the fire on the USS *Enterprise*, which started when a rocket was accidentally fired into aircraft on the tightly packed flight deck.

Another aircraft carrier suffered a major fire on 14 January. The USS *Enterprise* was participating in an exercise off Hawaii, prior to returning to Vietnam, when a Zuni rocket on a Phantom was ignited accidentally during start-up procedures. The rocket exploded among the tightly packed aircraft on the deck and the resulting fire took three hours to bring under control. Twenty eight men were killed and 15 aircraft destroyed and major repairs were necessary at Pearl Harbor, delaying the carrier's arrival on *Yankee Station* until 8 October.

Richard M Nixon was sworn in as the 37th President of the United States on 20 January and within a month the North Vietnamese decided to test his resolve. On 23 February they launched a nationwide offensive and although it was smaller than Tet 1968, US casualties began to increase. General Abrams, Commander USMACV, requested authority to bomb the enemy sanctuaries in Cambodia using B-52s and he was probably not a little surprised when Nixon gave his approval. In order to prevent more domestic dissent, the President directed that Operation *Breakfast* be kept a closely guarded secret and even the B-52 crews were kept in the dark about their targets, flying and bombing according to *Combat Skyspot* instructions. During the next 14 months the B-52s flew 3630 sorties against targets in Cambodia, dropping over 100,000 tons of bombs in

what collectively came to be known as Operation *Menu*.

The Marines finally received their first four AH-1G Cobras on 10 April, when they arrived at Marble Mountain to join VMO-2's eight UH-1Es and 23 OV-10s. By the end of the year the squadron was at its full strength of 24 AH-1Gs and was well pleased with its 'far-superior weapons platform', compared to the UH-1E. The one main complaint that the Marines did have though, was that the AH-1G only had one engine and with the amount of time that Marine helicopters spent at sea, two engines would be preferable. The Marines eventually procured the twin-engined AH-1J Sea Cobra and the first of these arrived in Vietnam for combat evaluation in February 1971.

By the summer of 1969 Nixon's policy of Vietnamization was under-way. Three VNAF squadrons had re-

ABOVE: ARVN troops waiting to move up to the forward areas prior to *Lam Son 719*.
LEFT: A smiling Captain Roger C Locher, rescued after evading the enemy for 23 days following his shoot-down near Hanoi. With him is 7th Air Force commander, General John Vogt.

tired their Skyraiders and converted to the A-37 ground-attack jet aircraft by July. Fifty-four A-37Bs were delivered to the 516th, 520th and 524th Fighter Squadrons and as more units converted to the type, the Dragonfly became South Vietnam's principal strike aircraft. President Nixon met President Thieu at Midway Island on 18 June to discuss the war, and the first withdrawal of 25,000 US servicemen was announced.

On 18 July the North Vietnamese released three US prisoners of war into the hands of an American anti-war group in Hanoi. The North Vietnamese warned the POWs not to cause them

ABOVE: A Cessna A-37B Dragonfly from the 8th SOS on a bombing mission.

any 'embarrassment' or they would retaliate against those left behind. However, the other POWs had urged the trio to speak out about their ill-treatment when they got home and at a press conference on 3 September Navy Lieutenant Robert F Frishman did just that. He announced that the POWs had been beaten, tortured, placed in solitary confinement, provided minimal medical care and otherwise mistreated. Ten days later the US Government, which had in fact known about the torture for at least two years, finally reported to the International Conference of the Red Cross meeting in Istanbul, Turkey, on Hanoi's gross violations of the Geneva Convention. The same day that Frishman held his press conference, Ho Chi Minh died in Hanoi, and a three day cease fire was observed in his honor.

From then on the treatment of the prisoners of war began to improve.

The first round of US troop with-drawals was completed by the end of August and on 16 September Nixon announced that 35,000 more troops would leave Vietnam by the end of the year. The North Vietnamese had not made any concessions as a result of the troop withdrawals, just as they did not when the *Rolling Thunder* campaign ended. The North Vietnamese con-tinued to drag their feet at the Paris peace talks, while October saw one quarter of a million anti-war protesters invade Washington D C. The war was being decided not in Vietnam, but on the streets of the United States.

As plans were being drawn up to expand the VNAF by 1100 aircraft and helicopters, the slow withdrawal of USAF squadrons began. The 8th Tactical Bomb Squadron deactivated and flew its B-57 Canberras from Phan Rang Air Base back to the United States

for storage on 6 October. The 8th, along with the 13th TBS which had deacti-vated in January 1968, were among the first squadrons to deploy to Vietnam in August 1964. Only one in three of the 96 B-57s assigned to the two squadrons survived to return to the States.

During October the 44th TFS moved its F-105s from the Phantom-equipped 388th TFW at Korat to join the 355th TFW at Takhli, thus consolidating all Southeast Asia Thunderchief assets at one base. The USAF presence at Pleiku and Binh Thuy was reduced to one squadron at each and Nha Trang Air Base was turned over to the VNAF. The 14th SOW and its units moved from Nha Trang to Phan Rang, where they were joined on 21 October by the first six AC-119K *Stinger* gunships of the 18th SOS. The AC-119K was modified from the AC-119G specifically for the truck-hunting role over the Ho Chi Minh Trail. The K model was equipped with two General Electric J85 jet engines which helped to keep the heavy gunship out of the way of the enemy AAA fire, while it engaged targets with its four 7.62mm miniguns and its two 20mm cannon.

The withdrawals continued in November and December with the 41st Tactical Electronic Warfare Squadron at Takhli RTAFB deactivating and redistributing its 15 EB-66C Destroyers among other units. The F-102 detachments at Udorn and Da Nang were withdrawn and the 609th SOS at Nakhon Phanom returned its A-26A Invaders to the States for storage. The last AC-47 squadron, the 4th SOS, deactivated and gave its gunships to the VNAF. Three of the type had been retained for base defense by the 432nd TRW at Udorn RTAFB and others were given to the Air Forces of Thailand, Laos and Cambodia.

With US troop strength down to 474,000, President Nixon announced in December that 50,000 more were to be withdrawn over the next four months. Thailand also announced

plans to withdraw its 12,000 man contingent, although the 50,000 South Korean troops were to remain for the time being. Despite the fact that most large Viet Cong and NVA regular units had withdrawn to their sanctuaries in Laos and Cambodia, US losses for 1969 stood at 9249 dead, 69,043 wounded and 112 missing. During the year 132,000 communists were claimed to have been killed, although 115,000 replacements had been infiltrated south at the same time. By the end of the year though, combat activity was at its lowest level since 1964.

1970 saw continued base reductions in South Vietnam and Thailand, and by the end of the year the Air Force would move out of Binh Thuy, Pleiku, Tuy Hoa and Vung Tau in South Vietnam and Don Muang airport and Takhli RTAFB in Thailand. On 12 January 1970 Ubon RTAFB was attacked by a small force of communist sappers who attempted to destroy aircraft with satchel charges. Five of the raiders were killed within a few feet of the *Blind Bat*

C-130s. Such attacks were rare and the aircraft returned to Okinawa in June.

The intensification of the air campaign against the Ho Chi Minh Trail through Laos, caused the North Vietnamese to seek alternative supply routes through Cambodia. Communist ships began using the port of Sihanoukville to unload supplies, which were then trucked to the supply bases along the South Vietnamese border. By the summer of 1969 enough supplies were getting through to support enemy activities in two-thirds of Vietnam and around 40,000 Viet Cong and NVA troops were in Cambodia, supplying arms and ammunition to the local communist Khmer Rouge insurgents. Prince Norodom Sihanouk had managed to keep his nation out of the

RIGHT: A Navy RA-3B from VAP-61 with a selection of the cameras which could be fitted.
BELOW: Information from the sensors sewn along the Ho Chi Minh Trail was relayed to Thailand by EC-121Rs.

ABOVE: ARVN troops display a captured anti-aircraft gun.

RIGHT: Interior of an AC-119G gunship showing the four SUU-11 Minigun pods.

conflict so far, by turning a blind eye to both American bombers and North Vietnamese supply convoys, but on 18 March that came to an end. General Lon Nol, the pro-western army chief of staff ousted Prince Sihanouk, closed the port of Sihanoukville and ordered the North Vietnamese out of the country. Fighting soon broke out between the North Vietnamese and the weak Cambodian Army. General Abrams asked for tactical air strikes to be used against the NVA in Cambodia, in addition to the Operation *Menu* B-52 strikes. On 24 April Operation *Patio* began with air strikes up to 18 miles inside Cambodia.

President Nixon was convinced that the North Vietnamese would not negotiate seriously until they accepted that America could defeat them on the battlefield and he believed that the time was right for a demonstration of his resolve. The President approved a cross-border offensive against the enemy sanctuaries in Cambodia; the main areas were in the *Parrot's Beak*, an area which juts into South Vietnam, a mere 33 miles from Saigon and the *Fishhook*, a curved piece of land which projects into South Vietnam 50 miles northwest of Saigon.

On 29 April the South Vietnamese Army attacked the sanctuaries in the *Parrot's Beak* and two days later the 1st Cavalry Division launched an airmobile assault into the *Fishhook* area. US Army helicopter gunships had a field day decimating enemy formations caught in the open, supposedly safe in their sanctuaries. Tactical aircraft, B-52 bombers and fixed-wing gunships flew in support of the ARVN and US ground forces. Air Force C-130s also flew 21 *Commando Vault* missions in which they rolled 15,000-pound *Daisy Cutter* bombs out of their rear cargo doors to blast enemy positions or create instant helicopter landing zones in the jungle. The campaign was a resounding success in the short term, with the capture of thousands of tons of enemy rice,

RIGHT: A Vietnamese O-1 FAC with target-marking rockets.
BELOW: This North Vietnamese unit claimed to have shot down 162 American aircraft.

ABOVE: A-4s launching from the port catapult on the *Oriskany* as A-7s wait for the starboard catapult.
LEFT: An unusual task for a CH-54; transporting a Navy river boat.

millions of rounds of ammunition and an estimated enemy casualty figure of 4800 killed. It was a major setback for the North Vietnamese and led to the reduction of US fatalities in South Vietnam over the following six months from 93 to 51 per week. In the long term, however, the invasion provoked a serious backlash of public opinion in the United States. Violent student demonstrations on the college campuses came to a head at Kent State in Ohio, where four demonstrators were shot dead by National Guardsmen. An anxious Senate passed the Cooper-

Church amendment which prohibited the use of American ground troops in Cambodia or Laos after 30 June. The US Army had no alternative but to withdraw and the last helicopters; a *Pink Team* of an AH-1G and an OH-6A from the 1st Squadron, 9th Cavalry, reported re-entering South Vietnam at 17.28 hours, 29 June. The air strikes continued though, with Operation *Freedom Deal* and 8000 sorties were flown in Cambodia up to February 1971. Over 40 percent of the sorties would be against targets outside the authorized *Freedom Deal* area of operations.

BELOW: Fighting the 'Secret War' in Laos; a Skyraider from the 1st SOS.

The 13th TBS returned to Southeast Asia on 15 September and brought with them 11 *Tropic Moon III* B-57G Night Intruder aircraft. They were based at Ubon RTAFB and became part of the veteran 8th TFW which had recently flown its 100,000th combat sortie. The *Tropic Moon* B-57Gs were equipped with forward-looking radar, infra-red and LLTV, plus a laser device. They were used for night and all-weather bombing missions over the Ho Chi Minh Trail and it is claimed that their accuracy was such that 80 percent of their bombs hit within 15 feet of the aiming point. They returned home in April 1972, having lost only one of their number, in a mid-air collision with an O-2A FAC in the darkness of southern Laos in December 1970.

United States Air Force units not actively engaged in combat operations in Vietnam began withdrawing from Thailand in Project *Banner Sun*. The main unit to be effected was the F-105 equipped 355th TFW at Takhli RTAFB, which ceased combat operations on 7 October. Soon the only F-105s left in Thailand were the *Wild Weasels* of the 17th WWS at Korat RTAFB which would remain until October 1974. The Thunderchief fleet had suffered heavy losses over the years; 344 had been lost in combat, together with 63 to other causes.

Other squadrons going home were the 22nd and 602nd SOS who redistributed their Skyraiders among other units before deactivating. They were joined by the 45th TRS which had first

deployed its RF-101C Voodoos to Vietnam in November 1961. They left Tan Son Nhut for Mississippi on 16 November and had lost 39 aircraft over their nine year deployment.

After three and one half years of combat operations, 2 Squadron Royal Australian Air Force lost its first Canberra bomber on 3 November. *Magpie 91* was on a *Combat Skyspot* mission in the Da Nang area and released its bomb load at 22,000 feet. The radar bombing operator was still in contact with the aircraft when its pilot reported that he was turning on a heading of 120 degrees. That was the last transmission received from the two-man crew.

Despite an extensive search, no sign was ever found of the missing aircraft.

There were now over 500 American prisoners of war located in various prisons in North Vietnam. Fifty were held at Son Tay prison, 28 miles northwest of Hanoi and in June 1970 the Joint Chiefs of Staff asked Brigadier General Donald D Blackburn, Special Assistant for Counterinsurgency and Special Activity, to formulate a plan to raid Son Tay and rescue the prisoners.

Just before midnight on 20 November one HH-3E and five HH-53 helicopters carrying 92 Army Rangers took off from Udorn in Thailand. Diversionary attacks were being launched all over North Vietnam while the raiders, flying below 500 feet, closed on the prison. Two *Combat Talon* C-130E unconventional warfare aircraft dropped napalm markers and fire-fight simulators on the nearby sapper school, as the HH-3E dropped into the small prison compound. The HH-53s landed outside the compound and after breaching the walls the Rangers began a systematic clearing of the cell blocks, killing every North Vietnamese that they met on the way. Within minutes they realized that all the cells were empty; the prisoners had been moved in July to another prison seven miles away and US intelligence had not detected the move. Twenty seven minutes after the first aircraft arrived over the prison, the raiders departed, blowing up the disabled HH-3E as a parting gesture. Despite the intelligence failure, the raid itself was a tactical success and had the prisoners still been there they probably would have been rescued. News of the rescue attempt soon reached the POWs and morale was boosted accordingly. The North Vietnamese were severely shaken by the raid and within days all the POWs in North Vietnam had been moved to two or three prisons in the Hanoi area. The resulting overcrowding of the cells was a blessing in disguise; some prisoners who had been in solitary confinement for five years were ecstatic to find that they now had a cellmate.

In December the *Igloo White* sensor relay aircraft were reorganized when the 553rd Tactical Reconnaissance Wing was deactivated on the 15th. The 553rd TRS absorbed the EC-121R *Batcats* of the 554th TRS, bringing its strength up to 12 and the QU-22B detachment at Nakhon Phanom assumed the identity of the 554th TRS. On the 28th the last USAF C-130A transport aircraft, from the 374th Tactical Airlift Wing, departed Vietnam for Okinawa They were no longer included in the MACV airlift structure.

Throughout 1970, 171 USAF aircraft had been lost bringing the total number to 1950, representing a cost of $2.5 billion. The number of combat sorties had been reduced substantially from 966,949, to 711,440, of which 30,000 were flown over Cambodia. The Pacific Air Force had been reduced by 19

LEFT: A pilot from B Company, 4th Aviation Battalion helps rearm his AH-1G.

146

ABOVE: A C-7 from the 459th Tactical Airlift Squadron following the transfer of the type from the army to the USAF.

tactical squadrons with over 500 aircraft and 32,000 personnel. In contrast the VNAF now had 728 aircraft in 30 squadrons and they flew a total of 292,523 sorties in 1970.

Following the loss of their supply routes through Cambodia the North Vietnamese intensified their activities along the Ho Chi Minh Trail and during the first six weeks of 1971 an estimated 31,000 NVA troops and 1800 trucks arrived in Laos. It was obvious that a dry-season offensive into South Vietnam or Cambodia was being planned, so President Nixon authorized a pre-emptive strike against the enemy bases in Laos. As Congress had prevented the use of American combat troops in Laos, the fighting would have to be carried out by South Vietnamese troops, with US logistical and air support. The ARVN forces consisted of three divisions, three Ranger battalions, and an armoured brigade, backed by one US Marine medium

transport helicopter squadron, the 2nd Squadron/7th Cavalry, and a number of other aviation units under the operational control of the 101st Aviation Group. Operation *Lam Son 719* was launched on 8 February 1971 with the objective of reaching the major NVA supply base at Tchepone, 22 miles inside Laos. The ARVN forces attacked along Route 9 with an armored column, supported on its flanks by infantry and airborne units air assaulted into position. Artillery fire-bases were established on the high-ground and the invasion force advanced six miles on the first day. The enemy soon reacted violently to the offensive and a month of heavy fighting ensued.

On 6 March two ARVN battalions in 120 UH-1H slicks made air assaults into Tchepone and captured the town with only light casualties. By now the overextended ARVN units were coming under increasingly heavy pressure as NVA reinforcements were committed to battle. Helicopter sorties were seriously affected by the bad weather and when they could fly, they were facing the heaviest anti-aircraft fire of the war. Lieutenant General Hoang

Xuan Lam, the ARVN Commander, faced with increasing personnel and equipment losses and worsening weather, ordered a fighting withdrawal. Such a maneuver is difficult even with well-trained, disciplined troops, and ARVN losses were heavy, both in manpower and equipment. Estimates put the ARVN losses at 7000 killed and an unknown number wounded. The enemy also lost around 20,000 tons of food and ammunition, 156,000 gallons of fuel, 1530 trucks, 74 tanks and 6000 weapons. The Americans, who had only been providing air support, lost 176 killed, 1042 wounded and 42 missing in action. The total of 1260 US casualties is not surprising considering that 107 helicopters were destroyed and over 600 damaged. Despite the cost of *Lam Son 719* it delayed the enemy offensive for a full twelve months and bought Saigon and Washington additional time to carry out the Vietnamization program. Within days of the end of the invasion President Nixon announced that 100,000 more US troops would be withdrawn by December.

By the end of 1971 the 5th Special Forces Group had returned home, to-

ABOVE: Lt Randall Cunningham and his Radar Intercept Officer Lt William Driscoll; the first and only Navy aces of the war.

gether with the 1st Marine Division, 1st Cavalry Division (Airmobile) less one brigade, 173rd Airborne Brigade and the Americal Division which was disbanded. In July, US troops would relinquish all responsibility for defense of the area just below the DMZ to the South Vietnamese Army and in November President Nixon announced that US ground forces in Vietnam were now in a defensive role, with offensive activities being undertaken entirely by the South Vietnamese.

With US air activity over North Vietnam largely confined to armed reconnaissance flights and the occasional reprisal raid and with a slackening of air support requirements in the South, due to the reduction in the level of fighting, attention could be focused on the Ho Chi Minh Trail. The cessation of the *Rolling Thunder* campaign meant that the North Vietnamese had plenty of AAA weapons to spare and the presence of the first SAM site in Laos was confirmed on 4 March, three miles west of the Ban Karai pass. An 0-2 FAC aircraft flying in that area on 26 April became the first US aircraft lost to a SAM over Laos.

During the annual May to October monsoon in Laos, when *Commando Hunt* operations diminished, the North Vietnamese maintained an above average level of activity in Southern Laos. They built 140 miles of new roads on the Ho Chi Minh Trail, bringing the total of single roads, multiple parallel routes, by-passes and spur roads to 2170 miles. By the end of the year 344 anti-aircraft guns and thousands of smaller automatic weapons defended vital points along the Trail. More SAM sites were constructed in Laos and on the North Vietnamese border and by rebuilding their air bases in southern North Vietnam, their MiGs could now challenge *Commando Hunt* aircraft.

The *Lam Son 719* offensive did not inconvenience the North Vietnamese for long. Four out of every five trucks were still slipping through the electronic sensor net and despite American spending of ten billion dollars a year on the aerial interdiction campaign the enemy strength in Laos stood at 96,000 by the end of 1971. Another 63,000 North Vietnamese were in Cambodia and 200,000 more in the South.

In June 1971 the last USAF 0-1 Bird Dogs were transferred to the VNAF. Since their arrival in Vietnam they had flown over 471,000 sorties. On the 26th the F-100 Super Sabres of the 35th

TFW at Phan Rang Air Base ceased operations. They were the last of the type in Vietnam and they departed for the United States on 30 July. The F-100s had flown 360,283 sorties since their arrival in 1964 and had lost 243 of their number.

The number of US bases in South Vietnam continued to reduce as units returned to the United States or relocated to Thailand. Bien Hoa was given over to the VNAF in August and Phu Cat followed in December, leaving only Da Nang, Cam Ranh Bay, Phan Rang and Tan Son Nhut. The VNAF also received the last USAF AC-119G gunships on 8 September, although the USAF retained its AC-119Ks for the time being. The improvement and modernization program for the VNAF continued at full speed and by the end of 1971 the VNAF had 1202 aircraft and 1109 aircrews. They had flown 524,000 sorties, 59,800 of which were combat sorties and had lost 57 aircraft during the year. The USAF was still bearing the brunt of the air war and flew

450,000 combat sorties during the year, losing 87 aircraft. The KC-135 tanker fleet performed 62,500 aerial refuelings and the tactical airlift system moved 2,282,000 passengers and 283,000 tons of cargo, despite the rundown of American strength. At the end of 1971 American military strength had declined to 156,800 and Australia, New Zealand and South Korea had all announced that their troops were to leave.

With the onset of the dry season in late 1971, the enemy strength in Laos and Cambodia began to increase. President Nixon warned Hanoi on 10 December that North Vietnam would be bombed if it increased the level of fighting as US troops were withdrawn from South Vietnam. Within a couple of months, events were to prove that, if they were indeed listening, the leaders in Hanoi paid very little heed to the President's warning.

Although the bombing campaign over North Vietnam had come to a halt over three years before, reconnaissance

BELOW: Captain Steve Ritchie, the first USAF ace of the war and Captain Charles Debellevue, a WSO backseater, the second.

flights still kept an eye on the enemy's progress in rebuilding its factories, transport systems and lines of communication. United States satellites, Lockheed U-2 and SR-71 spy planes and tactical reconnaissance aircraft such as the Air Force RF-4C and RF-101s and the Navy RF-8 and RA-5Cs provided daily updates to the overall intelligence picture. It soon became obvious that North Vietnam was stockpiling supplies, weapons and ammunition and increasing the number of men moving South, in preparation for a major offensive.

Although safe passage for the reconnaissance flights had been theoretically agreed at the Peace Talks in Paris, the North Vietnamese continued to fire on them. In the last three weeks of 1971, ten US aircraft had been shot down over North Vietnam and Laos. In retaliation and in an attempt to deter Hanoi from launching an offensive in 1972, President Nixon authorized Operation *Proud Deep*, the largest series of air strikes against the North since 1968. For five days from 26 December the American aircraft flew 1025 sorties against enemy airfields, SAM sites, POL storage areas, supply dumps and

truck parks below the 20th parallel. The North Vietnamese were undeterred; soon their long-range artillery began shelling ARVN outposts across the DMZ.

Ninety retaliatory raids were flown against North Vietnam during the first three months of 1972, compared to only 108 during all of 1971. The reconnaissance flights continued and on 19 January, while flying MiG CAP for a reconnaissance mission over Quang Lang airfield, Lieutenants Cunningham and Driscoll, flying an F-4J Phantom off the carrier *Constellation* made the Navy's first MiG kill in 18 months when they shot down a MiG-21. The Air Force had to wait until 21 February before an F-4D claimed a MiG-21 shot down; it was the first Air Force MiG kill in four years.

By the end of February, 10 of North Vietnam's 13 Divisions were poised to invade South Vietnam. Three were north of the DMZ, opposite Quang Tri province in northern Military Region I and one had infiltrated into the A Shau Valley, south of the DMZ. Two were in Laos opposite Military Region II and another had infiltrated through to Binh Dinh province near the coast. A further

three were in Cambodia, preparing to cross into Binh Long and Tay Ninh provinces, a mere 60 miles north of Saigon. Not much could be done to counter the enemy's invasion preparations because of the rundown of US air power in South Vietnam. The last Marine aircraft had left in 1971, most of the air bases had been handed over to the VNAF and only two aircraft carriers were present on *Yankee Station*. A single USAF squadron of A-37s remained at Bien Hoa and three Phantom squadrons and five AC-119Ks were still at Da Nang.

Most of the American combat troops had left Vietnam; the 101st Airborne Division (Airmobile) departed on 10 March, leaving only the 196th Infantry Brigade, the 3rd Brigade of the 1st Cavalry Division and a battalion from the 21st Infantry. Some Marine and Army helicopter units were still in-country, but on the whole the South Vietnamese were on their own. They cancelled all leave, accelerated their recruit training program and positioned their forces to meet the anticipated attack. The 3rd ARVN Division with two of its three Regiments consisting of green troops, was deployed just south of the DMZ and reinforced with two brigades of Vietnamese Marines.

The invasion began on 30 March 1972 when, under the cover of very low cloud ceilings and low visibility, 30,000 North Vietnamese troops, together with two regiments of tanks thrust across the DMZ into Quang Tri Province. The attack was co-ordinated with similar thrusts from Cambodia toward Loc Ninh and An Loc and from Laos toward Dak To, Kontum and Pleiku in the Central Highlands. The ARVN defenders were now facing conventional ground assaults, backed by masses of artillery and for the first time PT-76 and T-54 tanks. The weather was so bad that air support was limited and what did get through found itself opposed by very heavy AAA fire, including some from 85mm and 100mm guns. Mobile SAM sites soon appeared in the South, together with the new shoulder-fired SA-7 *Strela* heat-seeking anti-aircraft missile, effective up to 8000 feet. The force of the enemy attacks sent the ARVN defenders reeling and they began to lose ground as their American advisers tried to call in air strikes or direct artillery support from US warships offshore.

The day after the invasion started the 35th TFS at Kunsan Air Base in South Korea was ordered to fly its F-4Ds to Da Nang, to reinforce the 366th TFW which was still in residence there. The Marines were hot on their heels and two Phantom squadrons began deploying to Da Nang from Japan on 6 April. A third Phantom squadron followed on the 13th, together with a detachment of EA-6A Prowlers for ECM missions and two TA-4F Skyhawks to perform air-borne spotting of naval gunfire for ships of the Seventh Fleet. Finally in mid-May two Skyhawk squadrons arrived at Bien Hoa to join in the defense of An Loc. One of the squadrons was VA-311, the last Marine fixed-wing unit to have left Vietnam in May 1971. The Navy had reinforced its two aircraft carriers on *Yankee Station* with the *Constellation* and *Kitty Hawk* by 8 April and had ordered the *Midway* and *Saratoga* to join them. By late spring the six carriers, each with an air wing of 90 aircraft, were in action; the greatest number of the war.

Back in the United States the Tactical Air Command initiated a series of major deployments, known as *Constant Guard I-IV*. *Constant Guard I* saw the despatch of the 561st TFS and its F-105G *Wild Weasels* to Korat RTAFB where they joined eight EB-66 Destroyers from Shaw AFB in South Carolina. The 334th and 336th TFS followed with their F-4Es and all 36 aircraft were at Ubon RTAFB by 12 April. On 1 May *Constant Guard II* began and involved the transfer of the 58th and 308th TFS to Udorn RTAFB with their 36 F-4Es. *Constant Guard III* became the largest single move in the history of Tactical Air Command. On 7 May the 49th TFW began to deploy its four Phantom squadrons to Takhli RTAFB and was soon flying ground-support missions around An Loc and Kontum. Thirty-six C-130E Hercules transport aircraft from the 36th and 61st Tactical Airlift Squadrons followed next under *Con-*

ABOVE: An 8th TFW Phantom releasing Mk. 84 laser-guided bombs over North Vietnam.
LEFT: An AH-1G Cobra from the 71st Assault Helicopter Company, the *Rattlers*, with 7- and 19-shot rocket pods on the stub wings.

stant Guard IV. By 30 May the USAF Order of Battle in South Vietnam and Thailand consisted of 20 A-1s, 20 A-37s, 54 B-52s, 14 AC-119s, 14 AC-130s, 348 F-4s and 31 F-105s.

Strategic Air Command began a series of deployments of B-52D and G bombers to Andersen AFB on Guam during April and May under the code name *Bullet Shot I-V*. Some bombers were flying missions over Vietnam less than 72 hours after receiving deployment alert at their stateside bases and by 30 May 117 B-52s were on 'the Rock' as Guam was called by the bomber crews.

The B-52 was the only aircraft which could still bomb in all weathers during the first few days of the invasion. B-52s flew 132 missions in the first week and on 9 April they resumed bombing strikes against targets north of the DMZ. The underground fuel storage tanks and a railroad yard at Vinh were attacked by a dozen B-52s on the first day and targets over the month included the Bai Thuong airfield and the Haiphong petroleum products storage area, all struck as a part of Operation *Freedom Porch Bravo*.

Despite President Nixon's strong action following the invasion, the previous restrictions had still not yet been thrown out of the window. On 11 April, General John W Vogt Jr relieved General John D Lavelle as Commander, Seventh Air Force. General Lavelle had been accused of bending the rules of engagement and ordering protective reaction strikes against enemy anti-aircraft sites, ignoring the requirement from Washington that the AAA were supposed to fire at the US aircraft first. Reports on some of the strikes had been falsified and one of the intelligence specialists of the 432nd TRW complained to his Senator about it thus bringing about an enquiry. The incident was a prime example of the stupidity of the rules of engagement, in which a pilot could not hit a SAM site until it showed hostile intent and launched a missile at him. Within a few weeks the enemy offensive was in full swing and US bombers began destroying the same targets that Lavelle had been relieved for hitting.

Within days of the start of the invasion 12 firebases south of the DMZ had been captured and the 3rd ARVN Division began to retreat. When the weather improved, airstrikes managed to stall the enemy advance, but by 2 May the North Vietnamese had captured Quang Tri city.

In Military Region III, Loc Ninh was

overrun on 7 April by the 5th VC/NVA Division, while two more Divisions converged on An Loc. The enemy attacked the city on the 13th, but the ARVN defenders, supported by AH-1G Cobras from the 3rd Brigade, 1st Cavalry Division and intense air strikes, repulsed the attack. A second attack two days later was also halted, so the communists decided to lay siege to the city and starve the defenders instead. One enemy division maintained the pressure on the city, while another blocked Highway 13, preventing reinforcements reaching the city. Both airfields were out of action and with the AAA fire in the area, the only method of resupplying the defenders was by air-drop from C-130s.

In Military Region II two North Vietnamese Divisions attacked across the border from Laos and by 24 April they had captured Dak To. A third division had infiltrated across country to the coastal region of Binh Dinh

province, east of Pleiku. They captured several coastal towns and blocked the north-south coastal road before B-52 strikes stopped the drive, short of Qui Nhon. Following the fall of Dak To, the highways to Kontum were cut and two months of heavy fighting ensued while the city was supplied by air. The first major battle of Kontum occurred on 14 May, but was broken up by fighter strikes and three UH-1B gunships equipped with the new TOW missile. The tube-launched, optical-tracked wire-guided (TOW) anti-tank missiles were undergoing field trials and happened to be in the right place at the right time. By 12 June the TOW equipped UH-1Bs had destroyed 26 enemy tanks.

As the fighting continued around An Loc, Quang Tri and Kontum, President Nixon prepared to carry out the

---

LEFT: An Army O-1 Bird Dog at Vung Tau.
BELOW LEFT: Going home; Marine CH-53A Sea Stallions from HMH-463 make a last trip over Marble Mountain in May 1971.
BELOW: UH-1Es land at a fire base to support the 9th Marines.

threat he had made in December. On 8 May 1972 he went on television and announced that he intended to cut off the flow of supplies that had for so long, permitted Hanoi to continue its war in the South. Operation *Freedom Train* had begun a month earlier on 6 April, but was confined to attacks on targets below the 20th parallel. The new campaign was named *Linebacker I* and it commenced with Operation *Pocket Money* on 9 May. On that day three A-6 Intruders and six A-7 Corsairs from the *Coral Sea* shrieked across Haiphong harbor at 50 feet, released four 2000-pound mines each and escaped without a scratch. The mining of the North Vietnamese ports had a devastating effect on the communist war effort; 85 percent of the country's imports and all of its oil arrived through the port of Haiphong. With the ports closed the only other supply lines into the country were the railroads and eight major highways into China. These would all come under attack in September when Operation *Prime Choke* was launched against the railroad bridges in the buffer zone between the north and China.

On 10 May, three and a half years after President Johnson called a halt to the *Rolling Thunder* campaign, full-scale bombing operations over North Vietnam resumed. The *Linebacker* campaign was to differ from the *Rolling Thunder* campaign in a number of ways. For the first time the President was prepared to risk the wrath of the Soviets and Chinese, by attempting to isolate North Vietnam from external supply. He also relaxed the rules of engagement and gave the local commanders more latitude and flexibility in directing the air operations than before. Improved munitions were now available including Laser Guided Bombs (LGBs) and Electro-Optical Guided Bombs (EOGBs), which meant that difficult targets could now be struck with precision. The old policy of gradual escalation was not to be applied to this campaign; its impact was to be immediate and crushing. Lastly, President Nixon had the will to win and he wanted results.

The air battles of 10 May, the opening day of the campaign, merit a book unto themselves. Thirty-two

Phantoms from the 8th TFW at Ubon flew north; 16 were loaded with unguided 'iron' bombs and heading for the Yen Vien railyard north of Hanoi and the other 16, loaded with the new 'smart' bombs, were about to pay another visit to the Paul Doumer Bridge. Because of the extent of the air defenses over North Vietnam the strike aircraft were outnumbered by support aircraft. Eight Phantoms were to provide ECM chaff support, 15 F-105G Wild Weasels were along to handle SAM suppression and four EB-66s

would orbit for ECM jamming. MiG CAP would be provided by Phantoms from the 555th *Triple Nickel* TFS. One hundred and sixty SAMs were fired at the strike force, but the attack was carried out successfully and one span of the bridge was dropped into the river. To the enemy's surprise a second strike force returned the following day and dropped a further three spans, closing the bridge for the duration.

As usual, the chaff, photo, strike and escort flights on 10 May were under the control of *College Eye* EC-121s, call sign *Disco*, orbiting over Laos and the Gulf of Tonkin. The Navy's *Red Crown* control ship in the Gulf also provided additional warning of MiG activity and on that day there was plenty. The four Phantoms from *Triple Nickel*'s *Oyster* Flight ran into four of the 41 MiGs launched that day and despatched three of them in short order. Suddenly four more appeared and caught *Oyster One*, flown by Major Robert Lodge and Captain Roger Locher, in a stream of cannon fire. Major Lodge died as his aircraft exploded, but Captain Locher ejected safely and landed deep inside North Vietnam, where he evaded capture for an amazing 23 days until a combat rescue team brought him out.

While the raid on the Paul Doumer Bridge was going on, a strike force of Navy A-6 Intruders and A-7 Corsairs hit the Hai Duong railyard between Hanoi and Haiphong. Twenty-two MiGs engaged the strike force and their Phantom escorts and in the ensuing melee seven of the MiGs were shot down. Three of the MiGs were claimed by Lieutenants Cunningham and Driscoll, who already had two kills to their credit. As their fuel ran low and they headed toward the Gulf they were hit by a SAM missile over Haiphong and had to eject over the water. They were rescued by helicopter and returned to the *Constellation* where they were feted as the first American air aces of the Vietnam war.

Laser-guided bombs were used with great effect again on 10 June when the 8th TFW was at last given permission to attack the Soviet-built Lang Chi hydro-electric plant, 63 miles northwest of

Hanoi on the Red River. The plant was capable of supplying 75 percent of North Vietnam's electricity, but breaching the dam would have meant drowning 23,000 civilians. Three flights of four Phantoms with 2000-pound LGBs carried out the attack. The first flight blew the roof off, the second flight missed its target, the transformer yard, but the last flight put all of its bombs into the roofless plant, destroying the turbines and generators without putting even a crack in the dam.

By the end of June 106 bridges in North Vietnam had been destroyed, together with all the major POL tank farms and the pipeline running south to the DMZ. The remaining dispersed POL supplies now had to be moved by truck, putting a greater strain on the transport network. The invasion in the South had ground to a halt, largely due to the application of US air power, especially the B-52 bombers. The sieges of An Loc and Kontum had been lifted, although Quang Tri would not be retaken again until September. However, it proved impossible to throw the invading North Vietnamese divisions back over the border. Instead, as the fighting slackened, they established themselves in the countryside and waited for the Americans to return home.

Despite the intense fighting the Vietnamization program continued.

TOP LEFT: The *Fire Fly* night target detection system of a .50 caliber machine gun and a battery of lights on a UH-1D.
LEFT: HAL-3 UH-1 gunships patrolled the waterways in the Delta until January 1972.
RIGHT: A UH-1 under repair.

The last USAF C-123 Provider squadron transferred its aircraft to the VNAF in June and the 366th TFW moved its Phantoms from Da Nang to Takhli RTAFB. Project *Enhance Plus* began in

---

LEFT: WSO Harry Edwards of the 443rd TFS poses by his F-4, equipped with laser designator and 'smart' bomb.
BELOW LEFT: The Lang Chi hydroelectric power plant was destroyed by 8th TFW F-4s using LGBs on 10 June 1972. Breaching the dam itself would have caused thousands of civilian deaths and would have been likely if such an attack had been made with other means.
BELOW: A flight of USAF A-37s over South Vietnam in 1969.

September with the aim of building up the VNAF to an adequate level to conduct operations, after the remaining US aircraft and 43,000 advisers and administrative troops left the country. By November 288 more aircraft had been supplied to South Vietnam comprising 116 F-5s, 90 A-37s, 28 A-1s, 22 AC-119Ks and 32 C-130As.

As the *Linebacker I* campaign continued, the *Constant Guard* series of deployments recommenced with the arrival of two F-111A squadrons, the 428th and 430th TFS at Takhli RTAFB on 28 September. Three squadrons of A-7D Corsairs from the 354th TFW began to arrive at Korat RTAFB in October under *Constant Guard VI*. It

was the first appearance of the Air Force A-7s in Southeast Asia, and they replaced the F-4Es of *Constant Guard II*. The A-7Ds flew their first combat missions on 16 October and three weeks later were given the additional task of replacing the A-1 Skyraider in the *Sandy* escort role for the SAR helicopters.

In the meantime the North Vietnamese negotiators in Paris had convinced Henry Kissenger's negotiating team that they were willing seriously to discuss peace. As a result all bombing was halted above the 20th parallel again on 23 October and Kissinger confidently announced that 'Peace is at hand.' He should have known better.

Up to that point the *Linebacker I* campaign had been very productive. Hanoi was having tremendous diffi-culty obtaining enough supplies to keep going and the enemy's reserves were being used up at a rapid rate. One former aide to the Johnson administration remarked that *Linebacker* had 'a greater impact in its first four months of operation than *Rolling Thunder* had in three and a half years.'

During November the last US air bases in Vietnam were transferred to the VNAF. Now all combat missions would have to be flown from bases in Thailand. Above the 20th parallel the North Vietnamese took advantage of

BELOW: An A-7E (nearest) and an A-6A on a combat mission from the *Constellation*.

the bombing halt to repair the damage done over the preceding six months. The main lines of communication, particularly the railroads from China, were soon serviceable and newly-arrived supplies began to flow south again. By mid-December more MiG-21s had arrived at Gia Lam airfield, the monsoon season was approaching and the talks in Paris were getting nowhere. The peace talks finally collapsed on 13 December 1972, by which time President Nixon had had enough. He had been re-elected for a second term as President in November and with domestic problems mounting he wanted the war finished and the POWs returned. It was time to send the North Vietnamese a message that they would clearly understand, and that meant B-52 attacks.

6. From Victory to Defeat

At 14.51 hours local time, on 18 December 1972, Major Bill Stocker's black-bellied B-52D slowly lumbered onto the end of the runway at Andersen AFB on the island of Guam. As the nose of the giant bomber lined up with the white center stripe, Stocker advanced the eight throttles to take-off power. Black smoke spewed from the engines as water injection was added to increase the take-off thrust and the Stratofortress began slowly to accelerate. The engines roared as they sought to overcome the inertia of the 450,000-pound aircraft and the dip and rise of Andersen's switchback runway. The aircraft soon reached 'decision speed'; there was no turning back now and with all systems 'in the green'

Stocker eased back on the control column and *Rose I* took to the air. Seconds later it was over the ocean and another B-52 took its place at the end of the runway. Eighty-six B-52Ds and Gs took off behind Stocker, their destination – Hanoi.

The decision to launch Operation *Linebacker II* had been taken by President Nixon a few days earlier when he told Admiral Thomas Moorer, the Chairman of the Joint Chiefs of Staff, 'This is your chance to use military power to win this war.' He added melodramatically, 'And if you don't, I'll hold you responsible.' The restrictions were now finally lifted and Strategic Air Command's 155 B-52s on Guam and 50 more at U Tapao in Thailand were

being given the chance to achieve what seven years of war had failed to do; to bring Hanoi to its knees by the swift, massive application of airpower against the heart of North Vietnam.

As the 87 B-52s from Guam and 42 more from Thailand neared Hanoi the support forces began to play their part. Specially configured F-4s laid down chaff; EB-66s, EA-3s and EA-6s with ECM equipment helped to create addi-

PREVIOUS PAGE: A B-52 drops its bomb load.
BELOW: Three Navy Phantoms from VF-161 on the *Midway* and three A-7E Corsair II attack aircraft from the *America* over a target in North Vietnam. VF-161 downed five MiGs during *Linebacker*.

ABOVE: A B-52 refuels from a tanker aircraft.

tional clutter on the enemy radar screens and further hide the bombers; Navy fighter-bombers attacked coastal gun emplacements and SAM sites while Air Force F-4s, F-111s and A-7s attacked airfields and SAM sites along the B-52 ingress and egress routes; Wild Weasel F-105s searched for enemy radar signals, against which they would launch their Shrike radar homing missiles; EC-121s provided early warning to the F-4s flying MiG

CAP, of any threat by the North Vietnamese fighters; and out in the Gulf SAR helicopters waited, to provide recovery help if required.

The 129 bombers arrived in three waves, four to five hours apart and attacked the airfields at Hoa Lac, Kep and Phuc Yen, the Kinh No complex and the Yen Vien railyards. As the B-52s began their bomb run they were required to fly straight and level despite any threat from MiGs or SAMs. This was due to the stabilization systems of the bombing computers requiring a certain amount of straight and level

flight, to ensure that all the bombs fell on the military targets and not in civilian areas. Another reason was to keep the cells of three aircraft together to maximize the mutual ECM support benefits and to prevent any mid-air collisions.

Captain Hal Wilson in the lead B-52 from U Tapao reported 'Wall to wall SAMs up ahead' as he neared the outskirts of Hanoi. Shortly afterward his B-52D was hit by a SAM missile and destroyed, along with two other G models from Andersen. Despite the 200 SAMs fired at the attackers, 94 percent of the bombs were on target and one MiG that got too close was shot down by the tail gunner in *Brown 3*. By the time the strike force had returned to Guam, the B-52s participating in the next day's raid were preparing to depart.

On the 19th all three waves of bombers hit their targets and although some bombers were damaged, none was shot down. That all changed on the 20th. Ninety-nine bombers in three waves, with four hours between each, struck targets around Hanoi and Haiphong. This time 220 SAMs were launched and six B-52s were shot down by the enemy missiles. It was hardly

surprising because the same tactics had been used by the bombers each day. The bombers were strung out in 70-mile long formations and hours would pass between the arrival of the first and last aircraft over the target. They used the same routes, altitude and headings and the same post-target turning points. It was at the turning points and during the straight and level flight over the bomb release point that the aircraft were the most vulnerable, especially the G models with their weaker ECM equipment. Because the enemy SAM operators could predict the flight paths merely by watching the first cell pass

overhead, they could fire missile salvoes in the direction of the bomber stream, without having to activate their radars and invite ECM jamming or the attention of the Wild Weasels. It was even reported that some MiGs were flying alongside the bombers and relaying their altitude and heading to the SAM sites on the ground.

RIGHT: Painted bombs on the USS *Saratoga* on its last day in the Gulf of Tonkin.
BELOW: A KA-6D Intruder tanker from VA-165 refuels an EA-3B Skywarrior from VQ-1 over the South China Sea in September 1974.

F-4Es of the 388th TFW from Korat RTAFB refuel from a KC-135 before heading North on a MiGCAP mission.

On the 20th the bombers on Guam were stood down and the B-52Ds at U Tapao, with their more extensive ECM equipment, attacked Hanoi on their own. Two of the bombers failed to return. The U Tapao force went on their own again the following night, against the petroleum product storage areas and railroad support structures around Haiphong. This time they approached and departed along six different tracks over the Gulf and all cells completed their mission without loss.

The 23 December mission was flown by B-52s from both Andersen and U Tapao against the Lang Dang railyards 45 miles north of Hanoi and three SAM sites, 30 miles south of the city. This time though, the tactics were altered and the bombers made random changes in altitude and heading following bomb release and all aircraft returned safely. Similar tactics were used by 30 B-52Ds from U Tapao on Christmas Eve, when they attacked the Thai Nguyen and Kep railyards 40 miles north and northeast of Hanoi. For the third day running no aircraft was lost, but another MiG went down to the tail gunner of *Ruby 3*.

The bomber force had a well-deserved rest during the 24 hour Christmas Day ceasefire. The next day the most ambitious raid to date took place when 120 bombers in 10 waves, struck 10 different targets around Hanoi and Haiphong. In order to saturate the enemy defenses the first cells of each wave were to have the same time on target and all bombing would be completed within 15 minutes, with all aircraft varying their altitudes, ingress and egress routes to avoid the many SAMs directed at the bomber force. Out of the 113 support aircraft and 120 bombers, only two did not make it back. *Ebony 2* a B-52D was hit and exploded in mid-air and a damaged B-52, *Ash I*, crashed just short of the runway at U Tapao with only two survivors.

On the ground, the effect of the bombing raid was dramatic. In the 'Hanoi Hilton' the American prisoners

ABOVE: A USAF HH-53 refueling from an HC-130P in January 1973.

TOP RIGHT: 90 A-37s were given to the VNAF in 1972 under projects *Enhance* and *Enhance Plus*.

RIGHT: A VNAF F-5 from the 522nd FS at Bien Hoa begins a bombing run.

of war cheered wildly as the walls shook and plaster fell from the ceilings as the columns of B-52s rolled in. The terrified guards cowered in the lee of the walls, knowing that if the bomb line moved over a few thousand yards they would not live through the night.

A similar raid took place on Hanoi on the 27th, when 60 B-52s and 101 support aircraft attacked seven targets, releasing all their bombs in a mere 10 minutes. More SAMs were fired than the night before, but their aim was noticeably poorer. One B-52 was shot down over Hanoi and another made it back over the border to Thailand before its crew were forced to bail out. At last the weather had improved and the first bomb damage assessment photographs were obtained by *Olympic Torch* U-2R and *Giant Scale* SR-71 aircraft, together with drones launched by DC-130 *Buffalo Hunter* aircraft. The photographs showed that most of the bombers had been right on target, although one had missed Bach Mai airfield by 1000 yards and had destroyed a wing of the nearby hospital.

Sixty more B-52s attacked Hanoi on

LEFT: A captured B-52 crewman is paraded before the press in Hanoi.
BELOW: By July 1974, less than 8 of the 32 VNAF C-130s were serviceable daily.

the 28th and again on the 29th. The few SAMs that were launched exploded harmlessly away from the bombers and all returned safely. There were now no more worthwhile targets left in the immediate Hanoi or Haiphong areas and as the last B-52 bomber touched down on 'the Rock' on 30 December the order came down to cease bombing operations north of the 20th parallel. The *11-day war* had achieved its aim; the North Vietnamese wanted to talk again and serious negotiations began on 8 January 1973.

At last, through the application of its air power the United States now held the upper hand. The US position was accurately stated by Sir Robert Thompson, a recognized expert in counter-

RIGHT: A crowd gathers round the wreckage of a B-52 shot down on 28th December 1972.
BELOW RIGHT: A wing of Bach Mai hospital was destroyed during the 27 December raid.

insurgency warfare and head of the British Advisory Mission to Vietnam from 1961 to 1965,

In my view, on 30 December 1972, after 11 days of those B-52 attacks on the Hanoi area, you had won the war. It was all over! They had fired 1242 SAMs, they had none left, and what would come in over land from China would be a mere trickle. They and their whole rear base at that point were at your mercy. They would have taken any terms. And that is why, of course, you actually got a peace agreement in January, which you had not been able to get in October.'

Unfortunately, the United States failed to press home its advantage and demand more favorable terms, such as the withdrawal of all enemy troops from

---

LEFT: 432nd TRW MiG-killers Jeff Feinstein and John Madden meet Chief Gene Barnes who assisted both men as a Navy air controller on the USS *Truxtun*.
BELOW: An F-4B landing on the *Enterprise*.

South Vietnam. This was mainly due to the clamor of the American public against President Nixon's offensive stand. They wanted an end to the war and the POWs brought home.

The Peace Agreement was finally signed on 27 January 1973. South Vietnam's President Thieu was reluctant to sign the agreement and with good cause; there were 293,000 enemy troops still in his country. President Nixon advised Thieu that if he signed he would intercede more vigorously with Congress for continued aid to South Vietnam and pledged to react vigorously to any serious violation of the cease-fire by the North. On the other hand, if Thieu did not sign, the United States would cut off all aid to his country. Needless to say, President Thieu agreed to sign.

On 12 February 1973 Operation *Homecoming* began and the first batch of 116 POWs was released in Hanoi and by 29 March the last of the 591 POWs had returned home to an ecstatic welcome. At the same time operation

Endsweep began on 27 February when Navy CH-53s from Mine Counter-measures Squadron HM-12 started to clear the mines from Haiphong Harbour. It took until 27 July before the last mines were cleared from North Vietnamese waters.

Although the cease-fire agreement brought a halt to air operations over North and South Vietnam, the war still continued in Laos. During January 1973 American aircraft joined the Royal Lao Air Force in flying a total of 8000 sorties against the North Vietnamese and Pathet Lao troops. Finally the Pathet Lao and government forces agreed to a cease-fire on 22 February and all US tactical air support ceased on that day. Sporadic enemy violations of the cease fire led to additional B-52 strikes in February and April, but the bombing finally ceased on 17 April. It took the Pathet Lao a further two and a half years to gain complete control of Laos. The King abdicated in December 1975, ending a 600 year-old monarchy and the Peoples Democratic Republic

of Laos was proclaimed. The government's 185 US advisers were then replaced by 1500 Soviet technicians.

Two months after the cease-fire, the US Military Assistance Command, Vietnam, was disestablished on 29 March. By that date the last US aircraft and personnel had left Vietnam; the nearest USAF aircraft were now in Thailand.

Operation *Scoot* (Support Cambodia Out of Thailand) began in April to supply the Cambodian Government with food and ammunition. The North Vietnamese and Khmer Rouge forces were closing in on Phnom Penh so B-52s, F-111s, A-7s and AC-130s began to fly missions against enemy targets on the outskirts of the city.

The most crucial developments relative to the situation in Vietnam during 1973 took place in the USA. President Nixon was involved with the Senate Watergate committee and his administration had begun an irrevocable downward slide. In Congress the Case-Church Amendment was passed by the House and this directed that no more funds were to be used to support directly, or indirectly, combat activities in or over Cambodia, Laos, North Vietnam or South Vietnam by American forces after 15 August. The President would need to go to Congress for approval if he wanted to use American forces in Southeast Asia after that date. It was highly unlikely that Congress would give that approval and the North Vietnamese knew it.

The communists had no intention of honoring the Peace Agreement. Soon Hanoi began to re-equip and reinforce its units in the South, including deploying 20 more anti-aircraft regiments equipped with all kinds of guns, radars and SA-7 shoulder-fired missiles. These weapons afforded a degree of control over the airspace of Military Region I and much of II and III. This control increased until the VNAF could no longer operate over some areas. Under this ever increasing anti-aircraft umbrella the communists began a 'land and population grab' campaign. They over-ran ARVN outposts and isolated bases and even launched four division-size attacks during the year.

Congress passed the War Powers Resolution on 12 October 1973, which severely limited the President's tradi-tional freedom of action regarding the employment of the armed forces. It was now virtually impossible for President Nixon to enforce the terms of the Peace Agreement or the guarantee given to President Thieu.

The South Vietnamese Air Force was now on its own. By the end of 1973 it possessed a total of 2075 aircraft and had flown 458,000 sorties throughout the year. These had resulted in the loss of 185 aircraft, including 91 UH-1s, 26 0-1 Bird Dogs and 22 A-37s.

On 9 January 1974 there was the first mass student demonstration at the US Embassy in Thailand. Together with a recent change of government, this marked the beginning of the end of the US military presence in the country. By August all USAF flying units had left Ubon RTAFB and Takhli was returned to the Thai government in September.

The improvement program for the Khmer Air Force, known as Project *Flycatcher*, was terminated on 30 June.

BELOW: A North Vietnamese APC passes wrecked VNAF C-47s in revetments at Tan Son Nhut Air Base during the capture of Saigon.

The transfer of 23 T-28Ds and a smaller number of C-47s and 0-1s had, however, significantly improved the combat capability of the KAF.

The fate of South Vietnam was effectively sealed from July onward, as Congress began to cut back the amount of military aid to the Thieu government. The original request for aid worth $1600 million was eventually reduced to $700 million and austerity measures were introduced as a result. Over 200 aircraft were retired to flyable storage, including all the A-1 Skyraiders, 0-1 observation aircraft and C-7, C-47 and C-119 transports. The 36 F-5Es which the VNAF had only received in March, were returned to the United States. Troop reinforcement, resupply and medical evacuation were all seriously affected as helilift was reduced by 70 percent. The mobility of the units comprising the general reserve

RIGHT: An Air America Iroquois lands on the USS *Blue Ridge* during the final evacuation.
BELOW: A-37s from the 6th Air Division at Phan Rang and Phu Cat put up the best fight of the war, but it was not enough.

was greatly reduced as regular airlift was cut by 50 percent. The 32 C-130As were suffering from fuel leaks, wing cracks, spare parts shortages and cutbacks in flying time and only 4 to 8 aircraft were serviceable daily. Naval activities were reduced by 50 percent and river activities by 72 percent. The number of aircraft and vehicles awaiting spare parts began to rise drastically, as the stocks of fuel and ammunition began to run down. In the meantime enemy-initiated actions had increased by 70 percent over the previous year.

To add to South Vietnam's troubles, President Nixon resigned on 9 August and Vice-President Ford become the 38th President of the United States. South Vietnam had now seen the withdrawal of all US combat troops and air power and watched the run-down of USAF units in Thailand as America turned its back on the war. The war had cost America dear; 58,000 servicemen had died and the cost alone of the 3720 aircraft and 4868 helicopters lost to all causes came to almost $7 billion. Now US aid had been drastically cut and South Vietnam had to deal with a hostile Congress and a new President. The VNAF had lost 299 aircraft during 1974 and its strength was now down to 1484, with fuel and ammunition stocks for only 2 months of operations. They awaited the forthcoming North Vietnamese offensive with trepidation.

The beginning of the end came on 13 December 1974 when the enemy went on the offensive in Phuoc Long Province, 75 miles northeast of Saigon. Two North Vietnamese infantry divisions were used, together with supporting armor, artillery and anti-aircraft units and by 7 January 1975 the province and its capital Phuoc Long city had fallen. Although the province was not of strategic importance the loss of the first provincial capital in South Vietnam came as a shock to the population and armed forces. The victory was of great psychological and political significance to the North Vietnamese. There had been no reaction, let alone punishment by the United States; what more encouragement could the communists have asked for?

North Vietnam had 13 divisions already in the South on the eve of the final offensive and a reserve of seven in the North. Russia and China had provided them with enough supplies for a 15 to 20 month campaign and they now had secure lines of communication from Military Region IV in the extreme south of South Vietnam, clear to Hanoi.

The Vice-President of South Vietnam, Tran Van Huong, insisted on replacing General Nguyen Van Toan, the very competent commander of II Corps in December 1974, because of charges of corruption. His replacement by Major General Pham Van Phu contributed to the events that finally led to the collapse of II Corps, the capture of Military Region II and the rapid disintegration of the South Vietnamese armed forces.

The II Corps G-2 (Intelligence) warned the new Corps Commander that the North Vietnamese were preparing to attack the city of Ban Me Thuot. However, General Phu disagreed and the bulk of his forces were in the Pleiku area when the attack on Ban Me Thuot began on 9 March 1975. A very heavy artillery bombardment hit the city, followed by a tank and infantry assault and within 24 hours half the city and both airfields were lost. Despite President Thieu's order to the ARVN 23rd Division to hold the city at all costs and 200 close air support sorties flown by the VNAF, the city was in enemy hands by the 14th. The capture of Ban Me Thuot gave the communists control of Highway 14 to Pleiku and Kontum and Highway 21 to the coast. When Highway 19 was cut between Pleiku and Qui Nhon it became obvious that the North Vietnamese planned to isolate the forces in the Central Highlands and then attack each element in turn.

The same day that Ban Me Thuot fell, President Thieu held a strategic planning meeting at Cam Ranh Bay. The VNAF was not represented, although its airpower was the only means of off-setting the advantage that the North Vietnamese possessed in numbers and firepower. Thieu had considered withdrawing from Military Regions I and II and consolidating his forces in Military Regions III and IV, but it was too late for such a radical revision of strategy. He ordered General Phu to withdraw his forces from Pleiku and Kontum and move them 160 miles south-east to Nha-Trang, on the coast. This was in order to shorten the lines of defense in

LEFT: USAF HH-53s from the 56th SOW refuel on the USS *Midway* while waiting for Operation *Frequent Wind* to begin.

183

Military Region II and provide forces for a counterattack against the strategically important Ban Me Thuot. Instead of carefully organizing a gradual withdrawal, General Phu ordered a hasty pullout which cost II Corps the loss of 75 percent of its strength within 10 days.

The 6th Air Division was given 48 hours to evacuate all its aircraft and personnel from Pleiku to Phu Cat and Phan Rang. Although General Minh, the commander of the VNAF had not been forewarned about the withdrawal, he sent some C-130s to assist with the move. There was not enough time to ready all the aircraft for departure and 64 were left behind, including 21 A-1s, 11 0-2s and four 0-1s in storage. As news of the military withdrawal reached the civilian population of Pleiku a mass exodus began and troops and refugees streamed down the long-neglected Route 78 toward Tuy Hoa. Indiscriminate enemy artillery fire, ambushes and road blocks turned the retreat into a rout, with the survivors reaching Tuy Hoa on 28 March. Communist troops took over Pleiku and Kontum without a fight and Ban Me Thuot would not be recaptured because II Corps no longer

had any combat troops. Air America assisted in the evacuation of Pleiku; one of its C-46s (normal load 51 troops) flew out with 142 troops on board and took 90 miles to climb to 1000 feet.

The enemy offensive in Military Region I had begun on 19 March and within days they were in control of the whole of Quang Tri Province, next to the DMZ. By the 25th the tired remnants of I Corps' divisions were gathered in three enclaves along the coast at Hue, Da Nang and Chu Lai. The three cities proved indefensible and Hue was abandoned on the night of the 25th and Chu Lai on the 26th. The badly organized withdrawal from Hue was disrupted by enemy fire and any discipline remaining among the soldiers of the 1st Infantry Division soon vanished. Only a third of the troops reached Da Nang and these soon disappeared in search of their families and a way out.

The defenses at Da Nang soon caved in and during the morning of 29th March 10,000 defenders were evacuated by sea. The 1st Air Division managed to fly out 130 aircraft but 180 more and most of the division's personnel were left behind. Since the start of the offensive over half a million

refugees had converged on Da Nang and when the enemy began to shell the city panic set in. Any aircraft landing at the airbase was mobbed by hundreds of Vietnamese and it finally became so unsafe that the airlift was suspended. The President of World Airways, Ed Daly, took the last evacuation flight into Da Nang, but instead of picking up refugees, 270 soldiers from the Black Panthers, one of the Army's toughest units, fought their way onto the plane. A frustrated soldier outside threw a grenade at the wing and the explosion jammed the flaps open and the undercarriage down. Four soldiers rode in the wheel wells to Saigon, but one fell to his death on the way.

On 26 March General Frederick C Weyand, the US Army Chief of Staff arrived in Saigon to meet the US Ambassador and President Thieu. General Cao Van Vien, the chairman of the South Vietnamese Joint General Staff, asked the American delegation if B-52s could be used to bomb enemy troop concentrations. He was informed that the US Congress would be unlikely to approve any new US intervention.

The North Vietnamese leaders, initially surprised at the speed of the South Vietnamese collapse, now committed their reserve divisions. With 325,000 enemy troops advancing southward through Military Regions I and II the coastal cities, Qui Nhon, Nha Trang and Cam Ranh all fell one after another. Some heroic fights were put up by small ARVN units resisting North Vietnamese troops pushing south on Highway One or coming out of the Highlands. The 6th Air Division which had withdrawn from Pleiku to Phu Cat and Phan Rang eventually put up the best fight of the war. Its A-37s flew an all-out effort with some pilots loading their own aircraft as ground staff fought as infantrymen after the ARVN pulled out. Eventually Phan Rang was overrun on 16 April; Xuan Loc would be the last point of defense.

As the fate of South Vietnam was being decided, a tragedy occurred

BELOW: Cambodia: Marines prepare to be picked up by CH-53s from Phnom Penh, during Operation *Eagle Pull*.

during Operation 'Babylift.' On 4 April a USAF C-5 Galaxy transport aircraft carrying 326 orphans from Saigon for adoption in the United States, crashed less than a mile from Tan Son Nhut airport. The cargo door had blown out shortly after take-off and the rudder and elevator control cables had jammed, so that the pilot was unable to bank the aircraft except by changes of power. He attempted to return to the airport, but could not line up with the runway and crashed, killing 206 orphans and their escorts.

In Cambodia the war was also coming to an end. The communist forces had cut off the capital, Phnom Penh, from external resupply and had been laying siege to the city since January. President Lon Nol left the country on 1 April and with the final collapse imminent the US Embassy began evacuating its staff. Operation *Eagle Pull* began at dawn on 12 April when the first of 8 Marine CH-53 helicopters landed in a football field at Phnom Penh and began to load 82 Americans, 159 Cambodians and 35 foreign nationals. As the last helicopter took off two and one half hours later, a rocket exploded in the field. Before it was out of range the CH-53 took a hit in its tail rotor from a

12.7mm machine gun, but the badly vibrating machine made it safely to Ubon RTAFB. Five days later the city fell and Cambodia began to slide slowly back into the dark ages.

Following the loss of Military Regions I and II the VNAF flew around 180 sorties each day, mostly against defensive positions instead of the enemy convoys now moving bumper to bumper down coastal Highway One. Over 150 bombing sorties were flown by C-130s carrying pallets loaded with 55-gallon drums of fuel oil or pallets rigged with 3 or 4 bombs, to be dropped from 15 or 20 thousand feet. On nine occasions a 15,000-pound Daisy Cutter bomb was dropped and when the first one fell on enemy positions some four miles from Xuan Loc, the entire city shook as if rocked by an earthquake and all the lights went out. The explosion destroyed the headquarters of the NVA 341st Division and rumors began to spread that the B-52s had returned.

The last ditch effort to defend Saigon took place east of the city at Xuan Loc between 9 and 22 April. If Xuan Loc was overrun the airfield, depot and arsenal at Bien Hoa would follow and to prevent that the VNAF flew 600 sorties in support of the defenders. On 23 April

the ARVN 18th Division, together with the 1st Airborne Brigade, extricated themselves and carried out an orderly retreat from the city. As the enemy flanked Xuan Loc and came within artillery range of Bien Hoa Air Base, all operational aircraft were flown out to Tan Son Nhut and Binh Thuy. For all practical purposes the war was over with the loss of Xuan Loc, although the VNAF still had 976 operational aircraft, including 92 A-37s and 93 F-5s.

On 20 April USAF C-130s and C-141s began airlifting Americans and South Vietnamese refugees out of Tan Son Nhut airport. The following day President Thieu resigned and transferred the presidency to Vice-President Tran Van Huong. On the 27th three rockets hit Saigon, the first to do so in three and one half years. More were to follow and soon artillery shells began to fall around the airport. The next day five captured VNAF A-37s carrying 250-pound bombs, attacked the airport, destroying three AC-119s and several C-47s.

General Duong Van Minh was sworn in as President on the 28th, but he would not be President for long; 15 enemy divisions now encircled Saigon and time was running out. In the early hours of the 29th the airport came under fire again and a USAF C-130 was destroyed on the ground. As the enemy artillery scored a direct hit on the main fuel depot VNAF aircraft began to take-off and head for Thailand. At least 132 VNAF aircraft were flown to U Tapao in Thailand, including A-37s, A-1s, three AC-119s and at least two dozen F-5s, one of which carried two pilots instead of the usual one! A handful of VNAF pilots fought to the end. One AC-119 which had been patrolling the perimeter of Tan Son Nhut all night landed to refuel and rearm and took off again just before daybreak. At 07.00 the gunship was hit by an SA-7 missile and plunged to the ground in flames.

With the runway at Tan Son Nhut closed by enemy fire, US Ambassador Graham Martin gave the order to evacuate all US personnel from Saigon and Operation Frequent Wind began. It was not a moment too soon. During the afternoon of the 29th the first Marine H-53s and H-46s arrived, together with USAF HH-53Bs flown off the USS Midway. Over the next 18 hours these helicopters, together with Air America UH-1s, evacuated nearly 9000 Americans, Vietnamese and foreign nationals. Of these, nearly 2100 were lifted from the US Embassy compound alone.

Out in the South China Sea the US Seventh Fleet waited as over 50 VNAF UH-1s and CH-47s brought out more refugees. Even an 0-1 Bird Dog appeared with the pilot's family on board and made a successful landing on the

BELOW: A VNAF UH-1 is pushed off the *Blue Ridge* to make room for others to land.

ABOVE: A VNAF UH-1 ditches near the USS *Blue Ridge* as one of the ship's boats stands by to pick up the pilot.

RIGHT: Evacuees from Phnom Penh arrive aboard the USS *Okinawa*.

USS *Midway*. Many UH-1s landed on the command ship *Blue Ridge* and were then pushed overboard to make room for others desperate to land.

At 07.30 on 30 April 1975 the eleven Marine guards who had been beating back the crowds of Vietnamese at the US Embassy in Saigon, made a dash for the roof of the building. At the top of the stairs they turned and threw tear-gas grenades behind them and then climbed aboard a waiting Marine CH-53. The ramp came up and the helicopter lifted off. At 10.00 that morning the government of South Vietnam surrendered and the longest war in America's history came to an end.

Postscript

The fact that the North Vietnamese returned 591 American prisoners of war during Operation *Homecoming* in 1973 has allowed successive American governments virtually to ignore the 2500 other servicemen still unaccounted for. The majority of these were pilots. Half are listed as killed in action – remains not returned, and the rest as POWs or missing in action.

It is the opinion of the author that not all the POWs were released. Only 9 out of the 565 Americans missing in Laos were returned, and then only because they had been passed on to Hanoi, rather than retained as captives by the Pathet Lao. Nothing has ever been heard of the 76 servicemen still listed as missing in Cambodia, and some pilots, paraded before the television cameras after capture in North Vietnam, were not among the 591 prisoners returned. North Vietnam itself expected extensive war reparations and very likely retained a number of POWs as bargaining counters. The reparations were, for various reasons, never paid.

Historically, communist nations have never released all their prisoners of war following the end of hostilities. The Russians did not do so in 1945, nor did the North Koreans or Chinese in 1953. Some French prisoners taken by the Viet Minh at Dien Bien Phu did not return home until 1980. There is no doubt that the same thing happened in 1973.

In the last ten years there have been 770 refugee reports of sightings of individuals believed to be Americans. Of these, 166 are classified as 'Category One – Confirmed Knowledge' by the Defense Intelligence Agency. For some at least, the war is not yet over.

US Aircraft Losses, Southeast Asia, 1962-73

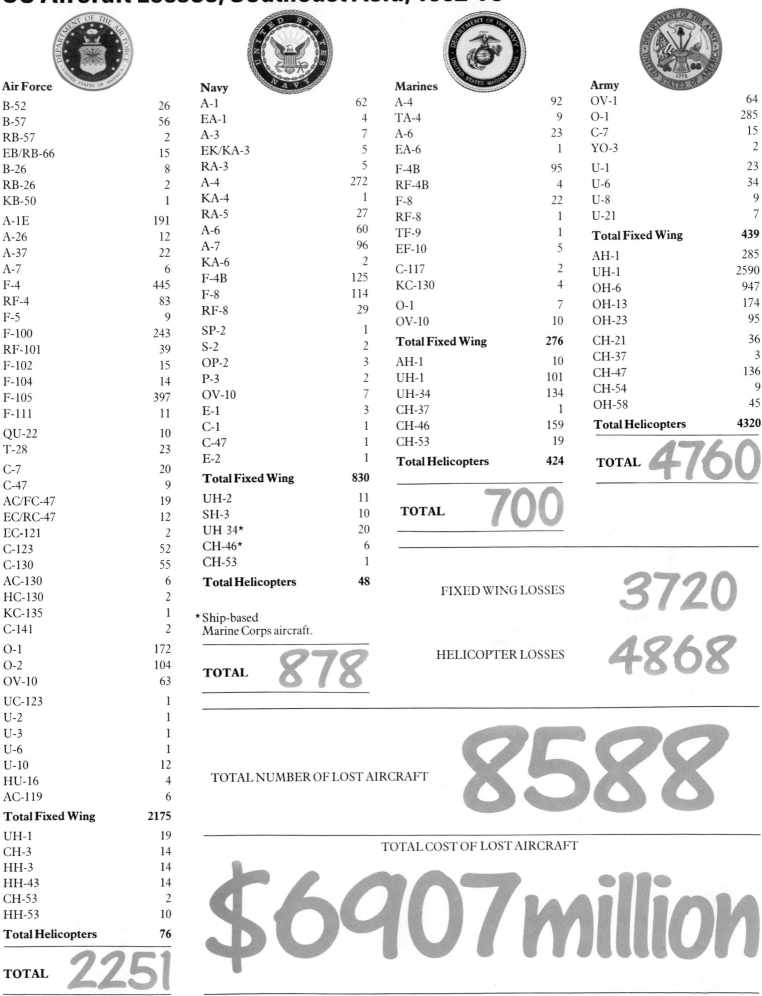

Air Force	
B-52	26
B-57	56
RB-57	2
EB/RB-66	15
B-26	8
RB-26	2
KB-50	1
A-1E	191
A-26	12
A-37	22
A-7	6
F-4	445
RF-4	83
F-5	9
F-100	243
RF-101	39
F-102	15
F-104	14
F-105	397
F-111	11
QU-22	10
T-28	23
C-7	20
C-47	9
AC/FC-47	19
EC/RC-47	12
EC-121	2
C-123	52
C-130	55
AC-130	6
HC-130	2
KC-135	1
C-141	2
O-1	172
O-2	104
OV-10	63
UC-123	1
U-2	1
U-3	1
U-6	1
U-10	12
HU-16	4
AC-119	6
Total Fixed Wing	**2175**
UH-1	19
CH-3	14
HH-3	14
HH-43	14
CH-53	2
HH-53	10
Total Helicopters	**76**

TOTAL 2251

Navy	
A-1	62
EA-1	4
A-3	7
EK/KA-3	5
RA-3	5
A-4	272
KA-4	1
RA-5	27
A-6	60
A-7	96
KA-6	2
F-4B	125
F-8	114
RF-8	29
SP-2	1
S-2	2
OP-2	3
P-3	2
OV-10	7
E-1	3
C-1	1
C-47	1
E-2	1
Total Fixed Wing	**830**
UH-2	11
SH-3	10
UH-34*	20
CH-46*	6
CH-53	1
Total Helicopters	**48**

* Ship-based Marine Corps aircraft.

TOTAL 878

Marines	
A-4	92
TA-4	9
A-6	23
EA-6	1
F-4B	95
RF-4B	4
F-8	22
RF-8	1
TF-9	1
EF-10	5
C-117	2
KC-130	4
O-1	7
OV-10	10
Total Fixed Wing	**276**
AH-1	10
UH-1	101
UH-34	134
CH-37	1
CH-46	159
CH-53	19
Total Helicopters	**424**

TOTAL 700

Army	
OV-1	64
O-1	285
C-7	15
YO-3	2
U-1	23
U-6	34
U-8	9
U-21	7
Total Fixed Wing	**439**
AH-1	285
UH-1	2590
OH-6	947
OH-13	174
OH-23	95
CH-21	36
CH-37	3
CH-47	136
CH-54	9
OH-58	45
Total Helicopters	**4320**

TOTAL 4760

FIXED WING LOSSES 3720

HELICOPTER LOSSES 4868

TOTAL NUMBER OF LOST AIRCRAFT 8588

TOTAL COST OF LOST AIRCRAFT

$6907 million

ACKNOWLEDGMENTS

The author and publishers would like to thank Design 23 who designed this book and Ron Watson who compiled the index. The majority of the illustrations reproduced come from the archives of the US Air Force, US Army, US Marine Corps and US Navy in the author's and publisher's collections. In addition the author would like to thank the following agencies and individuals for supplying the pictures on the pages listed:

Dr John Potes: 10, 12, 14, 16, 17.
Jim Wood: 14, 26(2), 33, 34, 40, 49, 52, 53, 59, 69, 131, 154-155, 166-167.
1st Lt M J Kasiuba: 2-3, 21, 37, 46, 47, 51, 59, 63, 75, 81, 91, 116, 137, 158-159.
Robert Livingstone: 29, 34, 95, 141, 157.
Nick Williams: 107, 111.
Ken Wilhite, Jr: 142.
Bruce Martin: 26, 65(2).
Richard S Drury: 145.
Ben Prieb: 43, 64, 69, 93.
John B Morgan 111, 146.
Lou Drendel: 58, 70, 74, 168.
Harry Sievers: 163.
Grumman: 68.
Kaman: 125.
Socialist Republic of Vietnam: 78, 79, 109, 112, 120, 121(2), 122, 180, 184.
Map, page 95, © Richard Natkiel.